Study Guide

A JOURNEY OUT

of the

WILDERNESS

Bringing Hope to Barren Destinies

Sherry Ward

A JOURNEY OUT *of the* WILDERNESS
Bringing Hope to Barren Destinies

Printed in the United States of America

ISBN: 978-0-9857942-3-1

Scripture references appear in the endnotes:

Scripture quotations marked "NKJV™" are taken from the New King James Version®. Copyright © 1982 by Thomas Nelson, Inc. Used by permission. All rights reserved.

Scripture quotations marked (AMP) are taken from the Amplified Bible, Copyright © 1954, 1958, 1962, 1964, 1965, 1987 by The Lockman Foundation. Used by permission.

Scripture quotations marked (NIV) are taken from the Holy Bible, New International Version®, NIV®. Copyright © 1973, 1978, 1984 by Biblica, Inc.™ Used by permission of Zondervan. All rights reserved worldwide. www.zondervan.com

Scripture taken from the NEW AMERICAN STANDARD BIBLE®, Copyright © 1960,1 962,1963,1968,1971,1972,1973,1975,1977,1995 by The Lockman Foundation. Used by permission.

Scripture taken from The Message. Copyright © 1993, 1994, 1995, 1996, 2000, 2001, 2002. Used by permission of NavPress Publishing Group.

Scripture quotations marked NLT are taken from the Holy Bible, New Living Translation, copyright 1996, 2004. Used by permission of Tyndale House Publishers, Inc., Wheaton, Illinois 60189. All rights reserved.

Cover Design & Interior Formatting | www.palmtreeproductions.com

Editor | Wendy K. Walters

Headshot & Makeup | Jacquelin Priestley

Website Design | Allyson Gideon

To contact the author or for bulk book orders:
www.WL2PL.com

DEDICATION

"A real friend sticks closer than a brother."
Proverbs 18:24b (NLT)

This book is dedicated to one of my best friends and prayer partners of twenty years, Melodie Fox, who through her own Wilderness experience has inspired me to keep going no matter what the odds.

Many of the revelations and insights were birthed in our time of prayer together. Melodie has a quiet spirit of wisdom that flows out of all that she does. Her dedication to continue to help me edit this book, even after her accident, is parallel to no other person I know. Her heart to help others through their Wilderness journey comes from a deep spring of compassion and humility. Her courage and tenacity in standing firm in the Lord has given me the fortitude to continue in my own journey out of the Wilderness. I admire her courage in the face of severe obstacles. Her story of hope is an inspiration to all who know her.

"For it is God who is at work in you, both to will and to work for His good pleasure."
Philippians 2:13 (NASB)

CONTENTS

DEFINING THE WILDERNESS

It is important to define the word Wilderness for a common understanding. The Hebrew word for Wilderness is *Midbar*, which means, "an uninhabited and desolate land.[1] The Free Dictionary by Farlex defines it as "an unsettled, or uncultivated region." The Wilderness conjures up for us all a barren, lonely place—a place of abandonment, or at best, a feeling of being lost, without direction. It is similar to the story of Hansel and Gretel; wandering, dropping bread crumbs, hoping to find their way back home.

The Wilderness is a very unsettling place. What was once *common* and *comfortable* to us has been exchanged for *confusion* and *stress*. For the purpose of this book, I choose to define the Wilderness as *"An extended trial that feels like it will never end! It is a significant trial that has a defined starting point and a defined ending point, and one that we only have to go through once."* There will be battles to be fought in the Promised Land, but they are completely different than our Wilderness experience.

Being in the Wilderness is not a quick trip. Nor is it something that lasts days or even weeks. Most likely it will last for months—probably for years! It is different than a trial, because a trial is typically thought of as a short-term experience, and usually has some sort of destination or direction in which we are headed. A trial often comes when we are moving forward, and all of a sudden we get hit with some unexpected, difficult situation.

The Wilderness is so very different because we are *called* to go into the Wilderness, even though at times it takes us completely off-guard and seemingly off-track. We no longer know where we are going and we can feel like a ship tossed about by the waves. We may feel like we are abandoned and forsaken, but God loves us so much that He wants to bring out of us those things that will be activated by the Wilderness experience.

The Wilderness is not about having a bad day, or even a bad week. It feels like a hard, dry, elongated journey, but God calls the Wilderness *good*. It is a place of activation of those things inside of us that have laid dormant. It is a deep work that the Lord is doing, and it is crucial for our development into our destiny. We may feel like it will never end, but God is in it and God will bring us through.

> **We may feel like it will never end, but God is in it and God will bring us through.**

Today, I believe the Body of Christ is going through a tremendous Wilderness experience, or what the Bible calls *shaking*. However, it is in this journey, this Wilderness, that we are receiving His *Kingdom*. The Bible says, "All of creation will be shaken and removed, so that only unshakable things will remain. Since we are receiving a *Kingdom* that is unshakable, let us be thankful and please God by worshipping Him with holy fear and awe."[2]

We are in good company in the Wilderness. Job endured a Wilderness experience where he felt alone and abandoned. His wife even chided him to curse God and die. Joseph felt isolated and alone in the bottom of a prison cell while he waited for his dreams to come to pass. Abraham felt unsettled and unsure as God told him to leave his familiar land to go to a place that he did not know, only to wait twenty-five years for his promised son, Isaac. We are not alone in the Wilderness; others have passed this way before. We can take encouragement and hope from their stories. Their testimony gives us confidence that what God has promised will surely come to pass.

I believe that God is raising up a remnant of believers in these last days. A remnant that will not only make it out of the Wilderness, but one that will learn their true authority to rule and reign. A remnant who receives all that God has for them. My prayer for you is to find the hope and the courage to continue this journey out of the Wilderness until you reach your own personal Promised Land.

ENDNOTES

1. www.blueletterbible.org.
2. Hebrews 12:27b-28 (NLT, Emphasis added).

ACKNOWLEDGEMENTS

"Let me say first that I thank my God
through Jesus Christ for all of you,
because your faith in Him is being talked about all over the world."
Romans 1:8 (NLT)

I dedicate and acknowledge that without God, I could not have produced this book. It was in collaboration with the Lord and in partnership with the Holy Spirit that this book came to fruition.

Thank you to my husband, Rolf. You supported me through the difficult process of writing a book. Thank you to my children, Megan, Caleb, and Bryce. You encouraged me to keep going no matter the odds. We have walked through this Wilderness journey together as a family, and you have served as an incredible inspiration to me of courage and child-like faith in God.

A special thank you goes to my review committee; Susy, Treseen, Allyson, Jackie, and Melodie who tirelessly helped me to edit the book. Your incredible insights and support were invaluable and much appreciated. Heartfelt thanks also go out to my endearing friends at the Monday night Bible Study. Thank you for praying over the book continually as I was writing it.

I would also like to express my appreciation to Deb. Thank you for giving me countless hours of your time in counsel in the development of the book. To Wendy, I appreciate your diligent work on the cover and formatting to get the book ready in time to go to print. Thanks to my parents, Del and Alyce. You supported me through all my endeavors.

INTRODUCTION

"Get out of the boat." I heard the words crystal clear. It was as if God Himself were sitting right next to me.

"Get out of the boat," He said again.

I knew exactly what God was telling me to do. I had felt Him tugging on my heart a few months earlier to start a new business, a corporation, and so I moved forward to begin the new venture. I was still trying, however, to straddle the new business along with the old nine-to-five to make sure I had enough money coming in for the family. This was traditional wisdom (so I thought), but God had other ideas. His idea of getting out of the boat meant quitting my job and letting go of the security of the past. I had to relinquish the old way of doing things. It was this *walking on water* position that landed me smack in the middle of my own personal Wilderness.

Many times after I had gotten out of the boat I said, "God, did I hear You correctly?"

Once I just finally asked Him, "Did I miss the boat?"

He quickly responded, "There is no boat. You are walking on water!"

Later He told me that the Wilderness experience was leading me into a *walking on water lifestyle.* I was learning a new way of doing business in the *Kingdom.*

I spent the next seven years, "walking on water," even though it felt more like I was *treading water.*

Getting out of the boat was a decision based on obedience that came with a price. This decision brought a new-found authority and power that rose up within me while I was on the backside of the desert. *The Wilderness is not a punishment, but rather an opportunity to proceed to the next level.* It is like a video game where we run the gauntlet and make it to the next level, only to encounter more challenges. The higher the level of play the more power we have in the game, and the more we have at stake. The Wilderness is a *qualifying process event* that, once we have passed the test, will allow us to move into a whole new arena.

My heart is for those of us who are "down for the count" and feel like giving up. We may be near the base of our mountain of influence, but instead of making progress in the climb, we find ourselves doing laps around the mountain, passing the same tree over and over again wondering, "When will this ever end?" My desire is to encourage you to keep going. You *will* make it through.

This book is not a "How To" book giving you ten easy steps for getting out of the Wilderness. Nor is it a book about all the things we must do while we are there. Rather, it is a book of insights and revelations that God has given me while I was in the Wilderness. It is the things that have helped to keep me going, *despite* the circumstances that surrounded me. It is a book to facilitate the transition into *Kingdom living,* and to help us continue moving forward when we think we cannot take one more step. When we finally do cross over into *Kingdom living*, we will see that the enemy has no hold on us. We are free—freer than we have ever been before! Even if the circumstances around us do not immediately change, they have lost their grip on us. That is true freedom.

3

We will make it through, but we will not be the same as when we went in. I promise you that!

One day in my prayer time I was thanking the Lord for all the *good* things that were coming my way in the future; all the *good* things that He had in store for me once I was out of the Wilderness.

He cautioned me and said, "Be careful of what you call *good*."

As I pondered this, I believe He was saying that our days in the Wilderness **are good**. They are all *good* because He is in them and has *good* for us at every turn, whether in the Wilderness or in the Promised Land.

Some days the battle may be raging all around us and it may take everything we have just to hold on to today— but really all we have *is* today. "This *is the day* the Lord has made; *let us rejoice* and be glad in it."[1]

Today declare that the Wilderness is *good*. We are not victims of circumstance. We need to take our today by the shoulders and declare it to be *good*. We have the power to command our day.

We need to take our today by the shoulders and declare it to be good.

4

I pray this book fills you with encouragement to make it through the Wilderness, and pours into you volumes of revelation to carry you on to the next leg of your journey.

ENDNOTES

1. Psalm 118:24 (NIV).

Today declare that the
Wilderness is good.
We are not victims
of circumstance.

CHAPTER ONE

LEAVING EGYPT

"Do not call to mind the former things, or ponder things of the past. Behold, I will do something new."
Isaiah 43:18-19a (NASB)

"An eleven day trip is all it would have taken the Children of Israel if they had gone directly through the Wilderness," I once heard a preacher say. "Only a few days in the Wilderness walking on a straight path, and they would have been out." The reality is that God does not always seem *efficient*, but in hindsight, His timing always proves to be impeccable. His way is not always direct, but always on course.

The Wilderness was not about taking the most *efficient* route or the *shortest* route. It was not simply about leaving at all! The Wilderness was about the Israelites *leaving* the mindsets they still carried from Egypt, and *bringing out* the character necessary for their destiny.

God had planned something greater for them than to simply have them travel from Point A to Point B. This was a transformation of their old ways of thinking and of the mindsets that had been instilled in them for generations. The Wilderness is a litmus test to expose what state of mind we are operating under, with the purpose of freeing us from wrong mindsets.

Many times our focus in the Wilderness is all about getting out. The "end game" in the Wilderness is not just about getting out. The Wilderness is a *process event* that forms the fortitude to fight and to discover the authority within us, in order to kick out the enemy in our land—whether in the Wilderness or the Promised Land. The Wilderness will develop in us the skill sets, and the authority that we have in Christ to kick the enemy off of our territory.

The Wilderness does not define us. *WE* define how we view the Wilderness and the *meaning* we attach to it. If we knew that

> The Wilderness has not changed, but we have changed the way we interpret it.

right around the corner was something very exciting and good, our attitude and expectation would be shifted tremendously. The *Wilderness* has not changed, but *we* have changed the *way* we interpret it.

Many of us have been called to a *process event* called the Wilderness. The purpose is to produce in us the necessary character to bring us to maturity in order to move us into our next assignment.

THE WILDERNESS IS A PROCESS EVENT

The Wilderness is a *process event*. God said in His Word that He would take the Israelites the long way around. "When Pharaoh finally let the people go, God did not lead them along the main road that runs through Philistine territory, even though that was the shortest route to the Promised Land. God said, 'If the people are faced with a battle, they might change their minds and return to Egypt.' So God led them in a roundabout way through the Wilderness toward the Red Sea. Thus the Israelites left Egypt like an army *ready for battle*."[1] They were ready for battle, but their mindset had not yet shifted to fight the battle. That is why the Wilderness is not about going from Point A to Point B. The Israelites were battle ready, but the first battle they needed to fight was an internal battle of wrong mindsets.

An internal fortitude is gained as we press through the Wilderness, and it brings us to a new level of authority for the next assignment we will be given in the Promised Land. This *process event* parallels the natural birthing process. A baby is conceived because of the intimate covenant relationship between a husband and wife. The baby then begins to grow inside the womb, and people begin to get excited about the development. Many people come up to the mother to *touch* her belly, filled with new life. They offer suggestions what to name the baby, or guess whether it is a boy or girl. After nine long months, the process of birthing begins as the child comes forth. As with anything that is being birthed, it carries with it the joy of the new delivery, but also a period of transitional pain. "A woman, when she gives birth to a child, has grief (anguish, agony) because her time has come. But when she has delivered the child, she no longer remembers her pain (trouble, anguish) because she is so glad that a man (a child, human being) has been born into the world."[2]

So it is with us and God. We come into an intimate covenant relationship with the Lord. The product of this relationship is the implanted seed of a dream or destiny that He has prepared in advance. The dream grows on the inside of us and many people want to touch it or get close to it. They may even try to name our "baby." We need to be careful of the people we allow in our life to come near our "baby." Just like Mary and Joseph had to protect Jesus from Herod because he was killing all the babies in the area, so too we need to guard the dream that God has entrusted to us. We need to be careful what we are speaking over our own baby. When Elizabeth and Zacharias were going to have John the Baptist, Zacharias spoke unbelief and the Angel shut his mouth so that he would not speak contrary to what was coming. Our goal should be to line up our words with what God is saying over us.

This birthing process is our Wilderness experience. The Wilderness is like transition labor in the birthing progression, when the pain intensifies and the contractions get closer together. Just when the mother is totally exhausted, completely spent, and can find no more strength to push—the joy comes as the new baby arrives!

The contractions are the many trials that increase and compound exponentially to push us to a new level that God has for us. It is unfamiliar and can be uncomfortable at times. During the birthing process we may cry out to God, "You did this to me!" But there is a joy that can be found in our Wilderness journey.

When the Angel Gabriel came to Mary and told her that she was to conceive Jesus in her womb, His first words were, "Greetings, favored woman! The Lord is with you!"[3] Mary told the Angel "May everything you have said about me come true."[4] We are highly favored to conceive the next part of our destiny. With this favor comes a trip into the Wilderness. Mary did not give birth in the comfort of her own home surrounded by her family and friends. Giving birth is not a comfortable experience. Mary was not only pregnant, but she had to ride miles on a donkey in the ninth month of her pregnancy, and then on top of it all, give birth in a barn surrounded by animals. Yet, she was highly favored! She had the joy of giving birth to baby Jesus. The wise men came and brought gifts, confirming many of the promises that had been spoken to her.

The Scripture says, "Can any good come out of Nazareth?"[5] Plenty! Jesus was the best thing that could have ever come into the world. We may ask, "Can any good come out of the Wilderness? The answer is still the same—plenty! The Wilderness will be the catalyst that propels us to the next level.

The Wilderness intensifies the gestation experience to birth the character in us not only to conquer, but to occupy and to rule in our Promised Land.

The Wilderness intensifies the gestation experience to *birth the character* in us not only to *conquer*, but to *occupy* and to *rule* in our Promised Land. In order to occupy and rule in our Promised Land, we will need to bring with us everything we have learned along the way in the Wilderness. We gain strategies and expand our understanding. Gifts we never knew we had come to the surface and we develop new skills all through our Wilderness journey.

It helps to think of collecting all these things in a spiritual tool box. As we go through the Wilderness, we are picking up different tools along the way and putting them in our box. Once we get to the Promised Land, we will need every tool that we have collected in the Wilderness to stay in that place to which He has called us. Each of us will pick up some basic tools that are common to everyone, but there are some specific tools that we will pick up that will be tailor-made for our own particular calling and destiny. This is one reason why the Wilderness looks different for each us, yet has some commonalities.

BID US TO COME

"Uncle...*uncle*...***UNCLE***," I said during one of the hard times in my own Wilderness experience. "I will do anything that You want me to do, just tell me what You want me to do, and I will do it!" I thought this was a good prayer because I was totally 100% committed and willing to do anything, but it was coming from a place of desperation and despair. It was not what He wanted. He wanted me to come to Him from a place of *trusted surrender*, not out of desperation.

He answered me and said, "You are asking the wrong question."

13

At this point I started panicking. I tried to figure out what *was* the right question that I was supposed to ask. I felt as if I was on some sort of game show. Finally it dawned on me that I should simply ask Him what the right question was.

I asked the Lord, "What *is* the right question?"

He said, "The right question is to ask Me what *I* am *about* to do, and how you can line up with what I am *about* to do."

This is a completely different perspective in yielding to God. He *bids us to come* and join Him in the work that He is *about* to do. When we ask Him what *He* is about to do, it puts us ahead of the curve. It is coming from an empowered state of being, and not a disempowered state. So many times after I started my company, I made my plans and basically asked Him to bless the work of *my* hands. My alignment was off.

The better choice was to ask Him what He was about to do, align myself with the Creator of the universe, and watch what He was about to do. He is extending an invitation for all of us to join Him in *The Work* that He is about to do to bring us into our fulfilled destiny. He is our King, extending His scepter for us to come into His presence and to join Him in what He is about to unfold. It may not be an easy trip, but it will always be a worthwhile one. The God of this universe *bids us* to come!

14

Peter spoke to Jesus when He was walking on the water and said, "If that is you Lord, bid me to come." Jesus bid Peter to come, so he got out of the boat and began walking. But then he took his eyes off Jesus and started to sink. Within a nanosecond, Jesus was there to extend His hand to help him up. So many times I have pictured this story. In my mind I saw Jesus ten feet away from Peter, but He was only an *arms length away*. Jesus reached out and grabbed Peter when He cried out to Him. He was so close that He was able to extend His hand and pull Peter up. The Bible says about the Israelites, "Yet they (are) Your people and Your inheritance, whom You brought out by Your mighty power and by Your *outstretched arm*."[6] God is just an *arm's length away* in the storm of our circumstances to help us walk on water.

Walking on water is His will for us. When we leave Egypt behind, walking on water is no longer just an exercise, it becomes a way of life—a way of living. Walking on water will be a lifestyle.

> God is just an arm's length away in the storm of our circumstances .

All of the disciples in the boat were *Christ followers*, yet Peter is the one that asked God to bid him to come. They were all *God-followers*, but only *one* had the courage to speak to the Lord and ask Him, "bid me to come." The challenge for us today is to ask God to bid us to come—come up to a higher level of living. Come up to a higher level of experiencing God. When we step out of the boat and begin to take those first steps, circumstances will arise to throw down the gauntlet and challenge us. The enemy uses these circumstances to discourage us, shift our focus to the past, look back, and sink into despair. Our job is to get out of the boat and keep walking. No matter what, we must keep our eyes focused on Jesus right in front of us. He is only an arm's length away.

Many times after I *got out of the boat* I said, "Did I hear God correctly?"

One time I asked God, "Did I just miss the boat?"

He quickly responded, "There is no boat. You are walking on water!"

Walk on the water by faith in the midst of the storm. Have the courage to believe. Doubt breeds fear, and fear leads to unbelief. Faith as small as a mustard seed is bigger than any element that would drag us down to defeat.

When we step out of the boat and walk on water, it puts us into a bigger place in the ocean. At the end of the movie *Finding Nemo*, Nemo and his friends were in a small fish tank. They made the water green with algae so that the owner would have to put them in small baggies while he cleaned their tank. They ended up escaping through the window to the ocean, but they were still floating around in their baggies bouncing around in the waves. So many of us are like the fish in *Finding Nemo.* We get out of our small fish tank, but we are still trapped in a "small thinking" little baggie and are not free to swim with the bigger fish in the ocean. We play it safe and can see all the other fish through our clear plastic baggie, but we are unwilling to get out and think big and swim in the ocean of God's revelation.

God has called us to *get out of the boat* and begin to walk on water. Then all of a sudden, circumstances begin to change. We start thinking, "Did I really hear from God? God was that really you? I would be better off going back to the old thing that I left behind—back to that dead end job I quit, or that relationship I left." Looking back to Egypt is very appealing. We easily forget the pain associated with Egypt.

When we choose to look ahead and not back, we are showing God that we trust Him. The question we need to ponder is: Do we trust Him? Do we trust Him through the Wilderness and barrenness of this season in our life? We do not know the end of our story yet. This Wilderness journey is only one chapter in our life. It is but a small part of a bigger story that He is unveiling for our lives. We cannot take just one chapter and say, "This is the way it will always be for me." No! This is one chapter,

17

and the rest of our story has not been played out yet. While we were still in our mother's womb, God had already written and produced the whole screen play of our lives. We are now the actors in our own movie. God is our director. Only He knows the plot. We need to ask God to direct the process and we will make it through.

Today choose to adopt a *walking on water lifestyle*. Abandon a lifestyle governed by the worldly system called mammon. The Wilderness can be a tough place to be at times, but it is the most rewarding and thrilling place at the same time!

Many people want God to call them by name and bid them to come, but this means a trip through the Wilderness. Getting out of the boat leads to our own Wilderness experience. How we handle our Wilderness experience will determine, to a great extent, our destiny. We will encounter several *qualifying*

> ## How we handle our Wilderness experience will determine, to a great extent, our destiny.

process events in the Wilderness. "For many are called, but few are chosen."[7] Many are called, but few trust God to lead them through the rough patches associated with the Wilderness.

God is bidding us as a loving Father to come into the Wilderness and into His training ground to teach us how to reign. There is an old poem called *Footprints.* It is a picture and poem of a man walking with Jesus on the beach and there are two sets of footprints, but then Jesus carries him and it becomes one set of footprints. This "*footprint*" season in the Body of Christ had its place and time, but we are entering into a completely different season in these last days. It is a season of training eagles how to fly—not for eagles to be carried everywhere. It is a season for us to spread our wings and fly.

If God is carrying us everywhere like the man on the sand, then we are not rising up in the authority that He has given us. God still comforts us, but if He carried us all the time, then we would not have the legs under us to do *The Work* of the calling that He has for our lives. This is a season to mount up with wings like eagles—not be carried everywhere. This is a season to grow up in all things and in all ways. Peter was on the water with Jesus right in front of him. Jesus did not carry him across the water, instead He was an arm's length away, training him to reach new heights in his faith. It is better to speak to the circumstances in our lives with faith and tell them to line up with the Word of God, while Jesus watches us like a proud father, than to continually live in fear asking Him to bail us out. We need to rise up into the calling that God has over our lives. If we do not know that calling, then in this season as we spend time with the Lord, He will reveal it to us.

The Lord bids us to come. At the beginning of the Wilderness, God is extending an invitation to join Him in an assignment that is strategic to our destiny. We can either choose to accept His invitation and move forward, or we can complain about our circumstances and circle the mountain one more time. By lining up with our assignment in faith, it will put us on the right trajectory to make it out of the Wilderness.

DO NOT LOOK BACK AFTER WE LEAVE EGYPT

When we leave our own personal Egypt, God does not want us to look back. Egypt may have good memories attached to it, or it may have some bad memories depending on what happened there. We may have been highly esteemed, at the top of our game—leader in our field. Perhaps we had great wealth and suddenly it was gone as we were thrust into the Wilderness. Moses forsook his life of wealth and privilege to be obedient to God and ended up in the Wilderness. On the other hand, the past may have carried bad memories. Maybe we were enslaved to debt, in an unhealthy relationship, or toiling to make ends meet like the Children of Israel. It may have been a place of heartache and pain, but in light of our present circumstances, we tend to forget the pain and romanticize the past. The Bible says, "If they had been thinking of the country they had left, they would have had opportunity to return."[8] The past, whether good or bad, is still the past. Whatever the case may be, leave it behind.

The Scripture says, "I press on to reach the end of the race and receive the heavenly prize for which God, through Christ Jesus, is calling us."[9] We need to keep our focus upward and forward. No reminiscing about the *good old days* when things were so much better. They probably were not really all that good anyway. "Because of the joy awaiting Him, He endured the cross, disregarding its shame. Now He is seated in the place of honor beside God's throne. Think of all the hostility He endured from sinful people; then you will not become weary and give up."[10] Jesus kept His focus towards the future and the joy that was set before Him.

He knew His purpose for being in the Wilderness and He pressed forward towards the destiny that lay ahead of Him. Being in the Wilderness carries with it the temptation to glorify the past—the old job that looks so good now, or the old relationship that was completely unhealthy. As we get older, our memory fades on those *good old days*, which were not always all that good. We can become emotionally attached to what *was*. This keeps us from what *is* and what *is to come*. The Bible says that we are going from glory to glory and from faith to faith.[11] Looking back prevents us from manifesting our future destiny.

21

BRINGING US OUT TO BRING US IN

God is bringing us *out* to bring us *in.*[12] God is bringing us out of our current position to make us ready to bring us into our own personal Promised Land. Abraham's father, Terah, was called to go to Canaan, which is the Promised Land of the Bible.

The Bible says, "Terah took Abram his son, and Lot the son of Haran, his grandson, and Sarai his daughter-in-law, his son Abram's wife; and they went out together from Ur of the Chaldeans in order to *enter* the land of Canaan; and they went as far as Haran and *settled* there."[13]

Terah had a mantle on him to go to the Promised Land, but he settled in Haran. A mantle was a robe or garment regarded as a symbol of someone's power and authority. It also represents a man's gift, or the call of God on his life. Terah settled for less than God's Promise. He stopped short before fulfilling where he was supposed to go. He did not make it through his qualifying process event and he settled for less that what God had for him.

The Bible says, "Now the Lord said to Abram, go forth from your country and from your relatives and from your *father's house*, to the land which I will show you; And I will make you a great nation, and I will bless you, and make your name great; and so you shall be a blessing; and I will bless those who bless you and the one who curses you I will curse. And in you all the families of the earth shall be blessed."[14]

Terah, Abraham's (Abram's) father, had a mantle that had been placed on him from God. Abraham assumed his father's mantle that was never fulfilled and went to the Promised Land. Sometimes there may be a mantle on a family that they were supposed to carry out, but they *settled*. The mantle is now on us to accomplish all that was intended in the beginning for our family. We are the new leader. We are the ones that need to lead the charge for our families. God has called *us out* to call *us in*. He wants us to leave behind the familiar and to go out of our comfort zone to a new place He is leading us.

As soon as Abraham was obedient and went out, there was a famine in the land. Abraham lands smack in the middle of a Wilderness experience and has to go to Egypt to stay awhile. So many times, we too, step out in obedience and end up in the Wilderness. Sometimes we may be carrying the fallen mantle of a family member, but we still end up in the Wilderness.

After the Wilderness experience, Abraham leaves Egypt and ends up back at square one. He was back at the exact place where his tent had been at the beginning between Bethel and Ai. God will bring us *out* to bring us back *in*. Yet, though we may be in the same place, when we return we are not the same. Our abilities and insight are not the same. Our understanding is not the same. Even our family is not the same. It is not about going around this mountain one more time. The circles become straight lines to lead us out of the Wilderness.

The things that God imparts to us in the Wilderness are at times only a three degree shift in our thinking. Three degrees is not much, but over a year three degrees is huge! It is the difference between going in a straight line and getting out of the Wilderness, or going around the mountain one more time.

In the Bible, "He (God) said to him (Abraham), I am the Lord who *brought you out* of Ur of the Chaldeans, to *give you* this land to possess it."[15]

God was saying, "I brought you *out* to bring you *in*."

The Bible also says, "Behold I am going to send an angel before you to guard you along the way, and to bring you into the place which I have prepared."[16]

Leaving Egypt behind is the first step in entering the Wilderness.

Leaving Egypt behind is the first step in entering the Wilderness. The Lord bids us to come, and we begin the journey as we follow Jesus' example of walking on water. This walking on water becomes a lifestyle. God is bringing us out to bring us back in, but when we come into our own personal Promised Land, we will come out with power and authority. We will have a new found confidence of who we are in Christ. Old mindsets have been jettisoned. We will never be the same. Have the courage to leave Egypt behind. God has great things in store for us as we continue this journey together.

OUR PRAYER TO GOD

God,

I am willing to leave Egypt behind. I give you this time in the Wilderness, and today I declare my days in the Wilderness to be good. I am willing to go through this process event and be here as long as it takes for You to work out of me the things that cannot enter the Promised Land. What are You about to do? How can I line up with what You are doing? (Selah...Wait on the Lord and spend some time listening to what He speaks to you. Then, in simple obedience, do it!)

Thank You that You have the best in store for me. I pray that You bid me to come. I am ready to receive all that You have for me in the Wilderness. I will make it through because You are bringing

25

me out, to bring me back in. Back in to a new place. Back in to a new position. Back in with a new-found power and authority like Jesus when He came out of the Wilderness.

I come to You with simple childlike faith and ask You to build my faith in the Wilderness. I receive the mantle that has been placed on me during this time. This mantle may have been meant for my family, but I will now lead the charge for my family, and give it to my children as a legacy and an inheritance for my children's children.

Lord, I ask You to bid me to come. Thank You for leading me into the Wilderness. I want to have a walking on water lifestyle and I am ready to embrace the journey today.

Amen

GOD'S PRAYER TO US

My Child,

Do not look back. Do not look to the "what if's"... just keep walking—just keep walking—just keep walking. For it is in the journey that My greatest work is being accomplished. It is in this Wilderness time that My work in you is being perfected—signs and miracles are just the icing on the cake. It is in the journey that My true work is being accomplished in you.

I love you with an unconditional love. That means there are no conditions attached—nothing you can do will move me anymore towards you than I am moved now. My heart, My ways, and My will are already with you in every way.

I bid you to come. Step out of the boat and trust Me with childlike faith. Simply trust—I will bring you out to bring you back in—to a wide and expansive place in the Promised Land.

Love,
Jehovah Shammah
The Lord Is There

STUDY GUIDE

1. In your prayer time with God, ask Him to reveal to you if there are any old mindsets that are holding you back in the Wilderness. What are they? Ask Him for forgiveness of those wrong mindsets, and begin the journey with Him to let those things go that are hindering you from coming out of the Wilderness.

2. The Bible says to offer Him a sacrifice of praise. Make a list of the "good" things that have happened in your Wilderness experience up to this point in time. This may be easier for some people than others. For some, this will truly be a sacrifice of praise. List as many as you can think of. Read them aloud every morning as a way to begin your day with praise in the Wilderness.

3. Ask God, "What are You about to do? How can I line up with what You are doing?" Listen carefully as He speaks to you, and then do whatever He says. The key is to not *only* ask the question, but to be *100%* obedient to what He tells you to do.

ENDNOTES

1. Exodus 13:17-18 (NLT).
2. John 16:21 (AMP).
3. Luke 1:28 (NLT).
4. Luke 1:38 (NLT).
5. John 1:46b (NASB).
6. Deuteronomy 9:29 (NKJV, Emphasis added).
7. Matthew 22:14 (NLT).
8. Hebrews 11:15 (NIV).
9. Philippians 3:14 (NLT).
10. Hebrews 12:2-3 (NLT).
11. 2 Corinthians 3:18.
12. Deuteronomy 6:23.
13. Genesis 11:31 (NASB, Emphasis added).
14. Genesis 12:1-3 (NASB, Emphasis added).
15. Genesis 15:7 (NASB, Emphasis added).
16. Exodus 23:20 (NASB).

How we handle the
Wilderness experience
will determine, to a great
extent, our destiny.

CHAPTER TWO

WHY ARE WE
in the
WILDERNESS?

*"Remember how the Lord your God led you all the
way in the desert these forty years, to humble you and
to test you in order to know what was in your heart,
whether or not you would keep His commands."*
Deuteronomy 8:2 (NIV)

"Testings come to find the Word of God operating in us," my friend Susy says. The definition of *testing* is, "The means by which the presence, quality, or genuineness of anything is determined; to check the quality, performance, reliability of something *especially before putting it into widespread use or practice.*"[1]

God tests us to bring out the quality of our character. Strength of character is necessary before He can put us into widespread use in a larger capacity. The Scripture says, "Enlarge the place of your tent; stretch out the curtains of your dwellings, spare not; lengthen your cords and strengthen your pegs."[2] How do we do this? In two words—The Wilderness.

The Wilderness is not a punishment, but an invitation to join Him in what He is about to do. and it expands us to receive that which is coming. The Wilderness is where this tremendous amount of growth takes place to get us to the next level that God has for us. But it does not always come the *way* we expected it.

PRUNING OR TESTING

I have heard it said many times of those who are going through a trial or a time of extended hardship, "God is just pruning me." This makes sense. Pruning away the places in us that keep us from bearing fruit is necessary for healthy growth. But pruning is *not* something God is *always* doing in our lives. In nature for example, a rose bush is only pruned once a year. For apple trees, there is a short window for pruning, and if they are pruned beyond that time, the tree can become endangered. We are not always in a season of pruning. Pruning is for a very specific time frame and season in our lives. For some, however, pruning becomes a daily occurrence and they use this as a constant complaint against the Lord. The Wilderness is definitely a time of transition and pruning, but it will *only* last a season.

TESTING US

Part of the definition of *testing* is "to check the quality of, performance of, reliability of something, *especially before putting it into widespread use or practice*."[3] God tests us in order to bring out those things that are inside of us with the end purpose of putting us into widespread use. Testing is different than tempting. It says in the Bible that God does not tempt us, but it does say that God tests us. Both may look similar, but the difference between the two is who is behind it—God or the enemy. The key is the *end goal*. The enemy's *end goal* in tempting us is to take us down and to get us out of the game. He wants to knock us out and disqualify our character so that we are not effective. God's *end goal* in testing us is to see what is in our heart in order to do good for us. The Bible says, "In the Wilderness He fed you manna which your fathers did not know, that He might humble you and that He might test you, *to do good* for you in the end."[4]

God already knows what is in our heart. When He tests us, it is for our benefit, so that *WE* can see what is in our *own* heart. This phrase "*to do good*" in the Hebrew means, "to make a thing good, right, or beautiful." Many times we look at testing as a necessary evil that God does in our lives, but this is *not* His motive. He is a good God *all* the time, and tests us with the end goal of bringing out the very best in us. That is His heart in the matter. That is His desire. We are not being dragged out to the shed to get a whipping. It is *not a punitive, judgmental type of testing*, but His heart is to see the good come out of us. That is the purpose of the test—not as a father who wants to catch us doing wrong, but as a loving Heavenly Father bringing to the surface those things that are already in our heart. He has implanted gifts and character traits in our lives. Often these lay dormant until stress or pressure bring them to the surface. This is what the Wilderness produces in us.

God's testing is different than Satan's temptation. Bayless Conley, pastor of Cottonwood Church said, "God never tests us in any area that Jesus already redeemed us from on the cross." For example, God never makes us sick to teach us a lesson, or to see if we have enough faith for healing. Jesus redeemed us on the cross. He died for our sins and was beaten for our *healing.*[5] The Bible says that by His stripes we were healed,[6] so God would never test us by making us sick. God's testing is meant to bring us to a new level of awareness of what He has already placed inside of us.

> **God's testing is meant to bring us to a new level of awareness of what He has already placed inside of us.**

34

One of my favorite poems is by Dr. Raymond Edman in his book, *The Disciplines of Life.* It talks about God's intention for testing us.

GOD KNOWS WHAT HE IS ABOUT

When God wants to drill a man,
And thrill a man.
And skill a man,
When God wants to mold a man
To play the noblest part;
When He yearns with all His heart
To create so great and bold a man
That all the world shall be amazed,
Watch His methods, watch His ways!
How He ruthlessly perfects
Whom He elects!
How He hammers him and hurts him,
And with mighty blows converts him
Into trial shapes of clay which
Only God understands;
While his tortured heart is crying
And he lifts beseeching hands!
How He bends but never breaks
When His good He undertakes;
How He uses whom He chooses,
And with every purpose fuses him;
By every act induces him
To try His splendor out—
God knows what He is about.

PROCESS EVENT

The Wilderness is our *process event* in order for us to move successfully to the next leg of our journey. This is similar to a computer that needs an upgrade. A message will appear on the screen of the computer and ask if we would like an upgrade for one of our software packages. Sometimes it will automatically give us an upgrade on its own, without our permission. If it upgrades on its own, then we have no control over when the process begins. At times we may get hit with a trial (upgrade process) we were not expecting. We know that we definitely did not click the *"yes"* button and agree to it. The process begins without our consent!

Sometimes, on the other hand, the computer will signal us to click *"yes"* and hit the button to begin. This would be the times when God calls us to obedience in a certain area, and we accept His offer, only to land smack in the middle of the Wilderness! On the computer, we are usually instructed not to touch any other buttons while it is downloading the improved version. Most of the time we need to wait—even if the screen goes dark, because the computer will need to reboot the system to activate the new software upgrade. The Wilderness is like that upgrade—with or without our permission—things are going to change!

While we are in this Wilderness experience (or computer upgrade), things around us may not make sense and it may carry with it a tremendous amount of pain from the loss of the old application. Just like a new program, we will need to "relearn" the new and get rid of the old ways of doing things. While the computer reboots, the screen may go dark. We may feel as if all of heaven has gone dark and extremely quiet as we wait on Him. But God is in the processes of *"rebooting us"* to give us an upgrade. This Wilderness time is an *upgrade and activation process,* but it might not come the *way* we were expecting. When we come out of our Wilderness experience, we will not be the same person anymore. We may not even recognize the person that we are becoming. It is worth the wait. Do not be tempted to hit "Ctrl/Alt/ Delete" and abort the process, or speed things along. This will only

The Wilderness time is an upgrade and activation process.

make the process slower. We cannot speed up our Wilderness journey. If we insist on doing it our way, we may find ourselves like the Israelites, going around and around the mountain.

The Israelites did not have faith to believe God would help them conquer the enemy in their Promised Land. They heard the report of the spies and they wept and mourned and said, "If only we had died in Egypt, or even here in the

Wilderness!"[7] God told Moses that *by the Israelites' own words they condemned themselves to die in the Wilderness.*[8] They would no longer be able to conquer their enemies and enter the Promised Land. Only Joshua, Caleb, and anyone in the younger generation would be able to enter. The people mourned greatly, and decided to take matters in their own hands. They heedlessly fought the enemy in the Promised Land by themselves, without Moses or the Ark of the Covenant. They ended up not only losing the battle, but the Bible says they were *beaten down*. At times we can be *beaten down* in the Wilderness, because we have not listened to the Lord's voice and what He told us to do. We can strike out on our own and try to *"make it happen,"* but in reality, the Lord is not going before us. When we try to push the keys on the keyboard ourselves instead of waiting on Him, we are on our own—out from under His protection, and open to enemy attack.

It is important that we obey what the Lord tells us to do in the Wilderness because timing is important. Taking our Promised Land is all in the timing, and one cannot be too early or too late. The temptation is to push through God's roadblocks or stop signs and *"make it happen"* ourselves. If we do this, we will surely get side-swiped, and it will take even longer to recover and get back on track.

NOW LET DEATH BECOME LIFE

Many times we are sacrificing things that are precious to us and allowing those things to die in our Wilderness, waiting for God to resurrect them and bring them back. It may be a job, a marriage, or our finances. God *is* in the business of resurrecting dead things, but His heart's desire is that the dead (unproductive things) in us are resurrected into a brand new thing. We become stronger and carry more authority coming out of the Wilderness. The key is to trust God through the disappointment.

> **God is in the business of resurrecting dead things.**

I believe the Body of Christ is going through a season of shaking which can lead to disappointment. Expectations are getting realigned. The Wilderness is a season of seeming disappointment. It is similar to when Jesus died on the cross and the disciples were grieved and disappointed. The disciples had given up everything to follow Jesus and wanted Jesus to be King. They *expected* to rule and reign with Him. They even fought among themselves about which one would sit at His right hand. They had placed all their faith and confidence in Jesus, and felt disappointed and let down when He died. After all, they had seen of countless miracles time and again, how could Jesus die? Even though He warned them, they did not understand that He was going to be killed. He was supposed to become King, and they had a certain *way* they thought that would happen. They went through utter *confusion*, *grief*, and *disappointment*.

The Wilderness can bring up similar emotions for us as well. The Wilderness is akin to the time between death and resurrection life. It may be the death of a dream or our own expectations. It is in this time between death and resurrection, that God is realigning our expectations. For example, Joseph probably thought his dream (where everyone in his household bowed down to him) had something to do with being in charge of his father's business, with everyone reporting to him in Canaan. But God wanted him in charge of the entire global economy of his day, doing his *Father's business*. Joseph's expectations had to shift into the bigger thing God was calling him to. God *WILL* come through for us— it just may look different than we *expected*. Our expectations will get realigned in the Wilderness.

When Lazarus died, Mary and Martha were devastated. Their *expectation* was that Jesus would come and heal their brother. They were faced with serious grief and disappointment when Jesus did not show up when they *expected*, and Lazarus died. It was four days between Lazarus' death and resurrection.

Once in my devotion time with the Lord, He gave me a Word for the following year. He said, "**Now let death become life. Let death be as nothing in the light of resurrection power.**" We need to press through our disappointments about *how* we *thought* God was *supposed* to come through for us and trust Him for the resurrection of the situation. It may not be a few days or few months, but possibly years. It may just be a trip into the Wilderness. But just like Joseph, there will be a resurrection of lost dreams, or a promotion—like Daniel after being in the lions' den, or David finally becoming king after years of hiding in the Wilderness from Saul.

The unconditional trust that we learn by having our *expectations* realigned in our own personal Wilderness will propel us to new heights with God. No more *fear of man*. No one will have a grip on us any more. When we have no fear of man, we can do anything for God!

ACTIVATION PROCESS

God uses the Wilderness to bring out our calling that has been placed inside of us since we were born. God leads us into the Wilderness to *test* us, *not* like a taskmaster, but to *bring out* what is already a part of us. All that we need for our destiny is already inside of us. The Wilderness is the *activation* process for our own spiritual DNA.

This activation process is like the story of the *Wizard of Oz*. The Cowardly Lion, Scarecrow, and Tin Man *already* possessed the very things they felt they lacked. They just did not know it. The Wilderness produced in them the characteristics they were outwardly seeking. The Cowardly Lion, by his very name, is an oxymoron. How can a lion be a coward? All lions have the innate characteristic of bravery. Throughout the whole movie, he was always a lion. He had never changed from being a lion, but he did not **see** *himself* as a brave lion with courage. He needed his courage activated by the trials he went through with Dorothy.

The Wilderness gives us illumination and allows us to see ourselves as God sees us. Jesus said that we would do even greater things than He did.[9] We are from the tribe of the great Lion of Judah. We need to begin to see ourselves as part of God's tribe. The point of being in the Wilderness and going through process events is for God to *illuminate* what *He has already placed inside of us*. He already sees it, *but we do not always see it* in us.

> **The point of being in the Wilderness is for God to illuminate what He has already placed inside of us.**

When the Cowardly Lion finally gets an audience with the Wizard, the Wizard said to him, "You already had courage *inside of you* the whole time." He gave the lion a badge to show the outward appearance of that which was always inside of him and now being manifested. It took the trials in the Wilderness while helping Dorothy to prove that courage was already inside of him. He just needed to believe it for himself. The Wilderness was the catalyst to bring to the surface his God-given courage. The same is true for us, the Wilderness is a time of activating those gifts inside of us, and allowing us to see them in ourselves. Many times others may see it in us, but we do not necessarily see it until the Wilderness activates it within us.

We are in the Wilderness to bring dormant things to the surface and to activate our authority in Christ. The activation comes through testing, and sometimes even through the death of a dream or expectation. God allows us to go through the process event of the Wilderness to produce in us a shift in thinking, and to bring us into a *Kingdom* mindset. We will not be the same coming out that we were when we went in. There will come a day when we come into our Promised Land and look back on our Wilderness journey with a special endearment. We will say, "It was all worth it!"

43

OUR PRAYER TO GOD

God,

I choose to rise up in the authority and power You have given me as a Child of God Most High. I bind a spirit of discouragement, and I loose a spirit of encouragement and hope. I will stand on Your promises every day. You give the "Yes," and I will give the "Amen!" I no longer declare things "gone" or "done" in the Wilderness, but stand in faith every day, that You carry the power of resurrection.

I will allow those things to die in the Wilderness that need to go, and believe You to resurrect and align expectations according to Your will. Bring forth and activate those things that are dormant so that I can see them too. Thank You for Your invitation to join You in what you are about to do, and to expand me so that I can receive all that You have for me.

Amen

GOD'S PRAYER TO US

My Child,

I am not a God who tests you to fail, but I am a God who tests you to bring out of you what I have already placed inside of you since the beginning of time. Shall you not see it? Shall you continue to keep so busy that "things" get in the way of you seeing it? The Wilderness is not a bad place. It is a time to strip away those things that you do not need in your life, and bring to the surface that which you will need in order to take the next step in My Kingdom, for My name's sake. Just like a knight that carries the flag of the country he is from, riding into battle with that flag, so too you are carrying my flag and my banner over you is love.

Those things you have given up for My Name's sake WILL be resurrected through the power of My Son, Jesus Christ. Let death become life. Let death be as nothing in the light of My resurrection power. Your situation may look "done," or there may be people speaking over you "gone," but I get the final word—I say when it is "finished!" I have great plans for you that have been in place since the foundation of the world. Let

45

Me reveal them to you, and trust Me to realign your expectation,
because I know what I am doing.

Love,
Jehovah Nissi
The Lord My Banner

God WILL come
through for us—it
just may look different
than we expected.
Our expectations
will get realigned in
the Wilderness

STUDY GUIDE

1. Is there anything in your life that you feel is either "gone" or "done"? What are they? Write them down. Give yourself permission to admit your disappointment and discouragement. Ask God to help you shift your expectation of these things. What is the Lord telling you about them? Write this down in your journal.

2. What is something in your life that you feel like God is "activating"? Perhaps it is only a faint stirring—something that you had deep down inside of you that is just starting to come to the surface. Write it down in your journal. Thank God, and ask Him to activate other things that are dormant in your life during this season in the Wilderness.

3. The Cowardly Lion went to the Wizard of Oz and asked him for "courage." What is **one thing** you wish you had more of in this Wilderness journey? Ask God for the thing you want. Write it down and pray about it often, until it begins to manifest in your journey.

ENDNOTES

1. Google Dictionary.
2. Isaiah 54:2 (NASB).
3. Google Dictionary.
4. Deuteronomy 8:16 (NASB, Emphasis added).
5. 1 Peter 2:24.
6. Isaiah 53:5.
7. Numbers 14:2 (NLT).
8. Numbers 14:28-29.
9. John 14:12.

CHAPTER THREE

CONTRADICTIONS

"God who...calls things that are not as though they were."
Romans 4:17b (NIV)

One of the litmus tests in the Wilderness is the contradiction test. First we get a Word from the Lord, or some sort of direction where we feel God is leading. Then we step out in obedience and think it is going to be a wonderful experience. After all, we were obedient—right? Then BAM! The backlash (contradiction to our situation) hits, and tries to knock us off our game. From Newton's Third Law, we learn that for every *action* there is *an equal and opposite reaction.* When we step out the enemy reacts. Immediately, circumstances look like the polar opposite to the direction God promised us.

Believe God even though contradictions arise in the Wilderness. Expect the contradiction and push through it. This is part of the testing process. God gives us a promise for a future that has yet to be manifested, so the enemy wants to cast doubt on God's promises when they are newly-formed within us. If he can shake us off God's promises before they are cemented, then he has won that round. Satan is a liar, but his lies are subtle at times. Satan tries to get his talons in our mind to fill it with doubt by asking us contradictory questions.

The enemy will say things like, "If you are so good with money, and God has promised you prosperity, then why are you in so much debt that you may lose your home?" ... "If you are really believing for healing, then why are you so sick?"... "If you have the gift of encouragement, then why are you depressed all the time?"

At one point in my journey through the Wilderness, we were struggling financially. Someone from my husband's work (at a fire station) took his picture without his permission, and put it on a website where they sell pictures for marketing purposes. A real estate firm bought that picture off the internet and created a pamphlet. His face was on the front cover of the pamphlet. The caption was: *"He can save many lives, but he cannot save his own home!"* This was a *directed* and *specific* attack on us financially and over our home. The enemy was trying to create fear in us that we would lose our home. The Lord had promised us prosperity, but the contradiction of the circumstances spoke to us daily and was exacerbated by the enemy posting it for the world to see on a pamphlet.

In football, the players do a lot of "trash talking" to the other players on the field. It is good offensive strategy to get inside their heads before a play is made. This was one of those moments when the enemy was "trash talking" to get us off our faith for our finances. It had to be the enemy, because the pamphlet was printed in a completely different state from where we live. How would we have even found out about it in the first place, if not for Satan's weapon formed against us? "No weapon formed against you shall prosper"[1] is the often quoted Scripture. The Hebrew word for weapon in this verse indicates a weapon specifically designed to take *us* out, not some generic weapon used for anyone.

The U.S. Air Force has heat-seeking missiles which are directed toward targets that are emitting infrared radiation. When we are on fire for God and seeking God with our whole heart, there is radiating from us an infrared tracker that the enemy wants to attack. He forms a weapon specific and tailor-made to target our personal weakness. Satan hand designs weapons that he knows will attack *us* at the very core. If the laser signal is blocked by a cloud, for example, then the weapon's accuracy will be greatly reduced. I believe one of our defenses to block these weapons is this "cloud" (of witnesses) we have concerning our faith.[2] The Bible talks about keeping our shield of faith up that will extinguish the enemy's attacks that come.[3] We need to be on guard for contrary thoughts that assail us, and always keep our shield of faith up. This will extinguish the flying missiles that come.

Faith is not a feeling. Faith is a choice. The Wilderness is about learning to make faith our choice every morning regardless of the circumstances around us. Rebuke aloud anything that is contrary to what *God* has spoken. That is how we "fight the good fight of faith."[4] The first word **fight** means, "to endeavour [sic] with strenuous zeal to obtain something."[5] The second part is **good fight**. The word **good** means excellent in nature and characteristics, and therefore *well adapted to its end*, and **fight** is the assembly of the Greeks at their national games.[6] This would be similar to our Olympics today.

We are in it to win it! We are well adapted to endeavor with strenuous zeal, or contend for our faith as though we have an audience cheering us on. "Therefore, since we are surrounded by such a great cloud of witnesses, let us throw off everything that hinders and the sin that so easily entangles, and let us run with perseverance the race marked out for us."[7] We have a crowd of people cheering us on in our faith. Our job is to hope against the hopelessness of our situation; to fight or contend for our faith, and to continue to believe and trust that God is big enough to handle it. The Wilderness is the crucible producing hope and faith in us which will sustain us in our journey out. Our faith...brings God glory!

JESUS IN THE WILDERNESS

Jesus had to face contradictions as well. Before Jesus went into the Wilderness, He was baptized in the Jordan by John the Baptist. God gave Jesus a Word from Heaven, just before He went into the Wilderness. As Jesus came out of the water from being baptized God said, "You are *My beloved Son,* in You I am well pleased."[8]

The very Word that God gave to Jesus *before* He went into the Wilderness was the exact Word Satan tested Him with *in* the Wilderness. Jesus *was* God's Son. When Satan came to Jesus in the Wilderness he said, "*If* you are Son of God, then command this stone to become bread,"[9] and "*If* you are the Son of God, throw Yourself down from here."[10] For two out of the three temptations, Satan tried to plant a seed of doubt that Jesus was *not* the Son of God, even though God had *just* spoken to Him when He was being baptized that He **was** His Son and that He was very pleased with Him.

The last temptation Satan brought to Jesus was when he took Him to the top of a mountain and offered Him all the kingdoms of the world. This was in direct contrast to the Word that Jesus received when God said He would give Him the nations as His inheritance. The Bible says, "You are my Son. Today I have become your Father. Only ask, and I will give you the nations as your inheritance, the whole earth as your possession."[11] This Scripture refers to God speaking over Jesus that He was His Son (Word at His baptism), and also that He gave Him the nations as His inheritance (His test in the Wilderness).

What the enemy was saying was in direct contradiction to what God had promised Jesus. The enemy challenges the very words God has spoken over us. It will not be something random, but we will be confronted in the very area of our anointing and calling *that has not yet been manifested.* Jesus was tested with "*If* you are the Son of God," before He had performed one miracle to

> **The enemy challenges the very words God has spoken over us. We will be confronted in the very area of our anointing and calling.**

prove who He was. He had only God's Word to stand on—the Word that Father God had given at His baptism before He went into the Wilderness. We need to take God at His Word because He faithful.

ABRAHAM'S CONTRADICTION

Abraham had his own set of contradictions. He was promised a son from his own body, and that this son would be the seed to many descendants—more numerous than the stars in the heavens. When Abraham first received that word he was old and so was Sarah, his wife. But after years of waiting (growing older and one step closer to the grave), God spoke a Word that seemed impossible! This Word contradicted their physical capacity to birth the promise God had spoken to them. But God is in the midst of the contradiction! Abraham received Isaac, his son of the promise, twenty-five years after God gave him the promise.

Later, God *tested* Abraham and told him to sacrifice Isaac. This was another contradiction. He could have said, "But God, why did you make me wait this whole time and stand on Your Word ... now you want me to give him up? This makes absolutely no sense!" Abraham trusted God through this huge contradiction. "It was by *faith* that Abraham offered Isaac as a sacrifice when God was *testing* him. Abraham, who had received

God's promises, was ready to sacrifice his only son, Isaac, even though God had told him, 'Isaac is the son through whom your descendants will be counted. Abraham reasoned that if Isaac *died*, God was able to bring him *back to life again*. And in a sense, Abraham did receive his son back from the dead."[12]

God's qualifying test looked like a huge contradiction. God's promise to Abraham was through Isaac, but Isaac was his only son. Why kill the very thing that God promised? God is not schizophrenic. God was testing Abraham to see if he was willing to trust Him completely *even in the midst of the contradiction and disappointment*. It was the ultimate test before Abraham was promoted. In the face of contradictions, Abraham hoped against hope[13] and trusted that God would be faithful. He continued to hope in God despite the fact that he was ninety-nine years old when he had Isaac.

The Wilderness is filled with contradictions. The circumstances around us may not look like all that God has promised us. It is at these key junctures that the question arises, "Do we trust God and believe Him anyway, or do we throw in the towel and call it quits?" In the Bible, when Peter's back was against the wall he said, "Lord, to whom

> **The Wilderness is filled with contradictions. The circumstances around us may not look like all that God has promised us.**

would we go? You have the words that give eternal life."[14] There comes a point in time when the decision needs to be made to believe *despite* the circumstances or the situation. Belief is a choice—not necessarily a matter of the heart at the beginning. In the Wilderness we may feel like our back is against the wall and disappointment is closing in on us like a dark cloud, but we will need to choose to believe *despite* all that is happening around us. God is the expert in resurrecting dead things!

BREAKTHROUGH EVENT

The contradiction is a *breakthrough event* to see if we will believe the Word God has spoken over us, or if we will shrink back. The Lord does not want us to shrink back, but to gain a new-found strength in the Wilderness. Once we press through, we will come out with a deeper revelation of who we are in Christ, and the authority that comes with it. The Bible says that when Jesus went into the Wilderness he was *FULL* of the Holy Spirit. But when he came out, He came out with the *POWER* of the Holy Spirit. We come out of the Wilderness having gained authority.

That is why the enemy does not want us to get out of the Wilderness. If he can keep us in small thinking, not pressing through and knowing the authority we have, we will be less of a threat to him.

The Bible says, "But my righteous one will live by faith. And if he shrinks back, I will not be pleased with him. But we are not of those who shrink back and are destroyed, but of those who believe and are saved."[15]

> **It is important not to look back at our prior history as a gauge for what we are about to do, because what God has in store—we have not done yet!**

We can take the Word that God speaks to us *before* and *during* the Wilderness, and use it as our shield of faith in the midst of the contradictions that come. It is important not to look back at our prior history as a gauge for what we are about to do, because what God has in store—we have not done yet!

It is imperative to trust God through our own set of contradictions. Our faith gets tested when circumstances are contrary to what God has spoken to us. It is only when our beliefs and obedience line up *despite* the circumstances that true faith is revealed. What we decide at this phase in the Wilderness will not only set our course, but our actual trajectory for the rest of the journey. Will we go round this mountain one more time, or will we learn the lessons and forge a path through it despite the circumstances?

HUMBLENESS

The Bible says that God led the Israelites into the Wilderness to humble them and to test them. Both of these words can have negative connotations. Many times when I hear the word *humble*, I get a picture of a brow-beating God who wants to "put us in our place," to be humbled before Him—The Almighty God. Nothing can be further from the truth.

The Wilderness strips away parts of our lives that need to go, or at best get shifted. This creates a huge space of vulnerability, and we can feel exposed. But vulnerability is not weakness. Being vulnerable is the first step towards humility. It can be a very uncomfortable place, but exactly what the Lord wants in order to place humility on us. Humility cannot be placed *over* all the baggage that needs to go, but only as we are stripped down to the bare essentials, can the covering of humility come upon us.

About halfway through my Wilderness journey, there was this humbleness that came upon me. It felt like a warm jacket on a cool winter day. It was one of the most wonderful experiences

I had in the Wilderness. I did not want to take off this new-found *jacket* of humbleness. Humility is not something we *put on*, but something that is *placed upon us* by the Lord at a certain juncture in our Wilderness experience. There is a humbleness that comes upon us so heavily that we want to just stay in that place forever.

I had never viewed humbleness that way before. True humility is completely different than what we may have previously thought. In some of the hardest parts of our Wilderness experience, when we are at our lowest and contradictions abound, God steps in and is the lifter of our heads. We come to know our rightful place, and we have a bigger sense of who God really is. That is when this *jacket* of humility comes down upon us. We need this *jacket* of humility, so that in due season when He exalts us, we will not be plagued by pride and fall.

The Bible says, "Humble yourselves in the presence of the Lord, and He will exalt you."[16] *Humility comes before the exaltation.* God wants to raise us up, but humbleness needs to come first so that we can stay at the top of our game when we get there and not be taken down by pride. The Bible also says, "...the humble will inherit the *land* and will delight themselves in abundant prosperity."[17] One of the meanings for *land*, refers back to the Promised Land.[18] Our journey through the Wilderness allows this humility to become a part of who we are, so that we will not fall prey to pride as He exalts us to our Promised Land in due season.

FAITH FOR TODAY ONLY

There were times in the Wilderness when I was humbled and was basically "down for the count." There were contradictions on every side. My faith was like manna—I only had enough for that day. I said, "God I can only think about today. I can only muster enough faith to stand for just one more day. I will not worry about tomorrow, but for today I choose to have faith and believe You." Sometimes I had to commit my faith to Him three or four times a day just to get through some of the rough patches in my journey. As long as it is called *Today*—Stand. Encourage one another daily, as long as it is called Today.[19]

Some days the battle may be raging all around us and it takes everything we have just to hold on to today, but really all we have *is* today. For God Himself says, "*This is the day* the Lord has made. We will rejoice and be glad in it."[20] Today declare that the Wilderness is *good*. We are not a victim of circumstance. The contradictions are not God's truth. We need to command our day. Take our *today* by the shoulders and declare it to be *good*. By doing this,

Take our today by the shoulders and declare it to be good.

we are creating a new mindset to put into the new wineskin that we are becoming.

CONFIDENCE REALIGNED

As contradictions assail us, many times our confidence gets stripped away. Our confidence may have been based on temporal or material things, or on our accomplishments instead of the Lord. When our confidence gets stripped away, it can leave us feeling vulnerable, but God is rebuilding us to be confident in Him. There is a shift that happens in the Wilderness as we move from resting on our own laurels, to trusting in the one true God to take care of us. It is a 100% yielding of the heart (*humbleness*) to do whatever God wants us to do, and to break off a spirit of control.

Humbleness allows us to hear what God is saying so that we can *partner with Him* in what He is about to do. Some only want to know Jesus by what He commands them to do, but He wants us to have more freedom than that. Still others run ahead like a thoroughbred horse, asking God to keep up with them, when God wants them to slow down and wait on Him. For each person this partnership with God looks different. Jesus had the perfect balance in *partnering with the Father*. Jesus said, "I tell you the truth, the Son can do nothing by himself. He does only what He sees the Father doing. Whatever the Father does, the Son also does."[21] Jesus was fully surrendered to the Father in complete humbleness.

Many times we do not even realize that our confidence lies in our own talents, because we did it in the "name" of God. For example, if we were in a ministry at church for years, or led a prayer group at a home, it is easy to take pride in *working for* God. *Working for* God is different than *working with* God or *partnering with God*. Doing "things" *for* God is not necessarily wrong, but we need to make sure God told us to do it. In one part of the Scripture it talks about people telling God that they had done *things* for Him, but He said He never knew them. Burn out is high among many in the Body of Christ who do and do and do.... Most things they expend energy doing are things that God did not even tell them to do in the first place! God wants us to do *only* what He has called us to do. He wants us to have laser-like clarity to focus on the *one thing* that He wants us to accomplish.

The end goal is not about works, or else we could have cause to boast.[22] It is about God's grace and His mercy *in* us and *through* us. It is not about doing great exploits *for God*, it is about God doing great exploits *through us*. Jim Caviezel said it best when making the movie, *The Passion of the Christ*. He said, "I did not play Jesus—He played me."

That is the shift that happens in the Wilderness. It is not us working for the Lord, but the Lord working through us as we fully yield to Him. When we yield, the spirit of control and unbelief is replaced by a mantle of humility and trust. That is where our confidence gets strengthened again.

For many years the Lord kept telling me, "Stop *doing* and *just be.*"

It took me a long time to figure out what He was saying. "What do you mean 'just be?'" I would ask.

I would sit there for five full minutes doing nothing and then say, "Okay God *I am* 'being.' Are we done yet?"

It took me many years to figure out how to "just be." "Just be" is a place where we let go of "doing" things for God's kingdom and find His rest. The "being" precedes the "doing".

There is a great line in the movie *Karate Kid* with Jackie Chan, when he says, "Being still does not mean doing nothing." We live in a society of proving our self worth by being busy. The busier we are the more important we are (or so we think). We are a go–go–go society. To "just be" takes much practice. It is a life study to "just be," but in order to *have* more, we must *become* more. The Wilderness is an inward journey of the soul to come through the turbulent circumstances in peace. Even though the circumstances may be swirling around us, we can rest in the eye of the storm. There is a safe haven in God's presence. A sweet spot in God that each of us needs to find on our own. It is an intimate encounter with the Lord that cannot be matched with any other natural experience.

The Scripture says, "Let us labor therefore to enter into that rest."[23] Labor to *enter* into His rest. The word *enter* in Greek means "begin to be."[24] In other words, labor to "just be," so that we can enter into His rest. It sounds odd—labor to rest, but that is what our goal should be. Not to labor in works, but labor to "just be" and enter into His rest. When Moses asked God who He was, He said, "I AM WHO I AM and WHAT I AM, and I WILL BE WHAT I WILL BE."[25] God did not give Moses a list of the things He *did* such as creating the Heavens and the Earth. He did not speak to Moses about His "doing." He addressed the essence of who and what He "IS." That is the same thing God wants for us; to simply have the essence of who He "IS"—like a sweet fragrant aroma. We are made in God's image, and He is causing us up to be more like Him in our Wilderness experience.

The Bible says, "Come to Me, all of you who are weary and carry heavy burdens, and I will give you rest. Take My yoke upon you. Let me teach you, because I am humble and gentle at heart, and you will find rest for your souls. For My yoke is easy to bear, and the burden I give you is light."[26]

God is at rest. He is the Alpha and Omega. He has already done the work. The work is finished. Now it is simply acting out what God has already accomplished. Labor to "just be" so that we will find His rest. As we enter His rest, a shift happens. It is like a horse and a rider. At first we were the rider and God was the horse. We rode Him here and rode Him there. We had a bit in His mouth leading Him wherever we went (or so we thought). We did great exploits for God, and had Him come along for the ride. Life was good and we were doing feats for the Lord and riding Him into the battlefield.

As the rider, we already knew where we wanted to go, so we steered Him in a direction that He may not have wanted us to go. Many times I have done things in the "name" of the Lord and ridden Him into a new adventure, only to find out that it was not such a great adventure after all. I have raced out ahead and then asked Him to "bless" (after the fact) certain business deals, or asked Him for favor on a situation without even consulting Him first. I am guilty of doing things in my own strength and then giving Him the credit: "Look how great God is!" when He was not even in the equation at all! I was not fully yielded and humbled, because I still had the reins of control in my hands. I had yet to give Him the reins completely and allow Him to break off the spirit of control.

Then through humbleness and being yielded to Him in the Wilderness, a shift begins to happen. He becomes the rider and we become the horse. What God does in the Wilderness is similar to a wild horse being broken. The goal is to break in the horse, without breaking its spirit. We are that spirited horse that God chooses to use, but He needs us under His submission in order to accomplish all that He desires.

God is inviting us to *join Him* in where He is about to go. He already knows where He wants to take us. He is training us to follow His lead. Now He is riding us (as the horse) into the battlefield and many times with blinders on our eyes so that we do not get scared. Blinders allow us to run free of distractions.

> God is inviting us to join Him where He is about to go.

One time I went to a conference where they talked about getting clarity, so I prayed to the Lord and asked Him to give me clarity and show me the "*box top to the puzzle.*" I was asking God for the *big picture* of what He had planned for my life. His response back to me was, "I am not going to show you the *box top to the puzzle* because you will try to control the whole thing

67

if I do." For months after He said that, I just gave up on clarity and threw the "baby out with the bathwater" so to speak. Since then, I have come to realize that He may not have shown me the box top to the entire puzzle, but I still needed clarity for the next specific steps in my journey. Clarity is still important. We can have clarity in our gifting, and clarity in what He has called us to do in *this* season. The more clear we are in what He has called us to do NOW, the more confident in Him we will become as we trust Him for the big picture.

> **We need clarity for the next specific steps in our journey.**

Not showing me the box top to the puzzle is similar to putting *blinders* on a horse. He did not want me to interfere or try to control the situation. He puts *blinders* on all of us at times so that we will not look to the left or to the right, but keep running straight ahead—running the race that He has put before us.[27] Since He is the rider and has the reins, He opens us up to run the race we were created to run and win. He is leading us and guiding us with a bit in *our* mouth. It is a humbling experience to be led by the bit, but the most exhilarating one too! A horse can sense when the rider has control and knows what he is doing. So too we can sense and have an expectation of what Rider-God is about to do, and know that He is in full control of where we are headed.

DREAMS GET REALIGNED

In the Wilderness, our dreams get realigned. One of my favorite quotes is from Charles Swindoll. He says, "We are all faced with a series of great opportunities, brilliantly disguised as impossible situations." We may see our dream one way, but God wants to take us through the impossibility of the situation to show off His glory. One time He told me, "Stop calling those things that *are* as though they *are*." What He was trying to get across to me, was to call those things that *are not* as though they *are*. He wanted me to believe for the impossible. We may have dreams that we think are great, but God has something even bigger and greater in mind. But we will need to let go of the dream first in order for Him to resurrect it.

> **We may have dreams that we think are great, but God has something even bigger and greater in mind.**

The vision or dream that God gave us may have an interpretation that we have not even considered. Our dream will be bigger than anything we could have accomplished on our own—and that is the point! There is a shift that happens that is exclusive to our Wilderness time. The Wilderness is an all inclusive package that entails humility, testing, and contradictions, but it is truly worth the trip. The Wilderness is a refining process like no other, which enables us to "partner with God" and hear His voice so that He can lead us into our destiny. We need to stand firm through the contradictions that will arise in the Wilderness, and choose to believe God at His Word every morning. Faith is a choice! Choose to believe!

OUR PRAYER TO GOD

God,

Today I choose to believe. I cannot think about tomorrow, but as for today, I choose to believe Your Word and Your promises. I take my today by the shoulders and declare it to be good. I make a concerted choice to have faith for today, despite the contradictions of the circumstances that daily beg for my attention.

I bind the spirit of depression and hopelessness that things will never change, and I loose a spirit of joy and hope, for You are guiding me in Your plan. Align my confidence in You as I learn to "just be" and to rest in your peace. I break off a spirit of control so that I can learn how to partner with You in all things and in all ways. No longer the rider, but now the horse—with You in command.

Realign and resurrect broken dreams. The dreams that have died in the Wilderness—resurrect them in Your power and authority. Thank You for a new level of humility that feels like a well-worn sweater on a cold winter day. Keep it continuously wrapped around me, because I want it to become a part of who I am.

I choose to press in today, despite the contradiction of the circumstances, and with simple childlike faith I say, "I believe."

Amen

GOD'S PRAYER TO US

My Child,

Keep that level of humility that I have placed on you. Yes, I the Lord have placed it on you for the greatness that is set before you.

Trust Me in the midst of your contradictions. Trust Me to come through for you. Trust Me to lead you in the way you should go.

Do not work for me, but let Me work through you as you learn to partner with Me every day.

Do not look back at your prior history as a gauge for where you are headed, because I have something in store for you that you have not done yet! Do not look to the left or to the right, for the plans I have are especially for you. Learn to "just be" and allow Me to be everything you need in this Wilderness experience. You will make it through.

Love,
Jehovah Shalom
The Lord Is Peace

STUDY GUIDE

1. What situation looks like a complete *contradiction* to what God has spoken over your life? Ask Him to show you some promises from His Word. Write them down in your journal, and then speak them aloud at least once a day to counter-attack what the enemy is trying to do.

2. Faith is a choice that we can make everyday. When you wake up each morning, tell God that you choose to believe Him at His Word. Your feelings may be screaming at you to the contrary, but commit to make this declaration **aloud** everyday.

3. What is one way that you can "Partner with God" today in what He wants to do? For example, if there is a decision that you need to make, instead of doing "pros" verses "cons" to make your decision, ask God what is His will in the matter. Write down any impressions, thoughts, or word pictures that come to your mind.

ENDNOTES

1. Isaiah 54:17a (NKJV).
2. Hebrews 12:1.
3. Ephesians 6:16.
4. 1 Timothy 6:12a (NASB).
5. Fight. *Strong's Exhaustive Concordance: New American Standard Bible.* Retrieved from http://www.blueletterbible.org.
6. Good Fight. *Strong's Exhaustive Concordance: New American Standard Bible.* Retrieved from http://www.blueletterbible.org.
7. Hebrews 12:1 (NIV).
8. Luke 3:22b (NASB, Emphasis added).
9. Luke 4:3b (NKJV, Emphasis added).
10. Luke 4:9b (NASB, Emphasis added).
11. Psalm 2:7b, 8 (NLT).
12. Hebrews 11:17-19 (NLT, Emphasis added).
13. Romans 4:18.
14. John 6:68 (NLT).
15. Hebrews 10:38-39 (NIV).
16. James 4:10 (NASB).
17. Psalm 37:11 (NASB, Emphasis added).
18. Land. *Strong's Exhaustive Concordance: New American Standard Bible.* Retrieved from http://www.blueletterbible.org.
19. Hebrews 3:13.
20. Psalm 118:24 (NLT, Emphasis added).
21. John 5:19b (NIV, Emphasis added).
22. See Ephesians 2:8-9.
23. Hebrews 4:11a (KJV).
24. Enter. *Strong's Exhaustive Concordance: New American Standard Bible.* Retrieved from http://www.blueletterbible.org.
25. Exodus 3:14b (AMP, Emphasis added).
26. Matthew 11:28-30 (NLT).
27. See Hebrews 12:1.

CHAPTER FOUR

PROVISION IN THE WILDERNESS

PART 1

"I will bless her with abundant provisions;
her poor will I satisfy with food."
Psalm 132:15 (NIV)

The Israelites' shoes and clothes never wore out. Forty long years they wandered around in the Wilderness, and their sandals never wore out! So, why did the manna spoil if they tried to save it for even one day? Why was the manna new every morning, except for the Sabbath?

When the Israelites' clothes did not wear out, God was showing them that He would not allow the enemy to have their provision or inheritance wear out or get destroyed. But through the manna, God showed them that His provisions are also new every day. Sometimes we have a part to play in gathering the provision, and to trust God that we have enough for the day. God has already gone before our situation and created the provision for us in the Wilderness.

God is not caught off guard about us being in the Wilderness, even though at times *we* might have been surprised at our circumstances. He has supplied the provision for us and sent it ahead of time. God told the Israelites to ask the Egyptians for gold, silver, and clothes for their Wilderness journey. "I will grant this people favor in the sight of the Egyptians; and it shall be that when you go, you will not go empty-handed. But every woman shall ask of her neighbor ... articles of silver and articles of gold, and *clothing*; and you will *put them on your sons and daughters*. Thus you will plunder the Egyptians."[1] They were instructed to put the clothes on their sons and daughters as a symbolic representation of their children's inheritance. It is interesting that God had the parents give their children the spoil of the garments (as a mantle) to foretell what was to come in the Wilderness. It was a prototype and foreshadow that their children would enter the Promised Land.

In my own Wilderness experience, there were material things and relationships that were dear to my children's hearts that were taken away, but I am standing on God's promises that my children's inheritance *WILL NOT* be stolen! I stand on the promises that God gave me during this time, and that my children will come into the full inheritance they have coming to them through their faith and His Word. The Wilderness brought out the *mama bear* in me towards the enemy, and nothing will prevent my children from entering into their own individual Promised Land; not as squatters on the land, but each with their own territory. "'There is hope for your future,' declares the Lord, 'and your children will return to their own territory.'"[2]

Our provisions *will* come in the Wilderness, but sometimes from unlikely sources. When the Children of Israel saw the bread from Heaven they called it manna. *Manna* means *"What is it?"* They did not have a clue about what it was, or how it got there. So it is with us in the Wilderness. God may provide in unusual and unexpected ways. It may not always be the typical nine-to-five J-O-B, but it may come from unforeseen places. My friend was in her Wilderness experience for seven years without a job, and God provided in unexpected ways, sustaining her when her husband, who was addicted to drugs, left her. People would come up and just hand her money, or someone would stop by with groceries. When her rent was due, she would often get a brown package in the mail with enough money to pay it!

> God may provide in some unusual and unexpected ways.

Another friend acted in obedience when God asked her to write a check to her church for the entire amount of her savings—$10,000. This was at a time when she was right in the middle of moving and splitting up with her husband. She was becoming a single parent when God asked her to give everything she had, right down to the last penny in her savings account. She was obedient to what God told her to do, and a couple days later a lawyer called her. He said he had a check waiting for her from a car accident settlement that was *TEN YEARS after* the fact! It was completely unexpected. She had no idea it was coming. The lawyer said he had been looking for her for years and had finally found her. When she went in to pick up the check, she looked down and the amount of the check was *exactly* $10,000. The *date* the check was written was the exact date she wrote the check to her church! She obeyed, and God provided for her in an extraordinary way. The key to our provision is to be obedient, even if it makes no sense.

God is not a respecter of persons. What He has done for others, He can do for you and me. But *obedience* is the key to

> **Obedience is the key to our provision, even if it does not seem to make sense.**

our provision, even if it does not seem to make sense. Our obedience may stretch us in ways that far exceed our comfort level. But that is the point! It is complete surrender and trust that God will provide for us. There are countless stories of God's provision. In this chapter we will recount some awesome *God Stories* to bring hope and encouragement through this Wilderness season.

PROVISION FROM THE HAND OF OTHERS

When David was in the Wilderness running away from Saul, God gave him provision through Nabal and guarding his sheep.[3] David knew the *sheep industry.* Tending sheep had been his primary job as a young lad, so God sent him to Nabal's flock to guard and keep them from harm. David was Nabal's personal "sheep body guard." In return for his flock's protection, as was customary in those days, Nabal was to provide for David and his men. Nabal was stingy and disobedient in providing for David, so God worked through Nabal's wife, Abigail, who made sure the men's needs were met.

There may be people who God has sent to provide for us in the Wilderness. Take comfort in knowing that even if those He sends are disobedient, it does not prevent Him from getting the provisions to us. Here is a story of how the Lord provided a car for my friend through the hands of others.

SANDRA'S STORY

When our second daughter was born, my husband and I were in agreement that the Lord was telling us to quit my job and stay home with the children. The only way we were going to do be able to do this was if it was God. I was making quite a bit more than my husband working at an aerospace company. We were getting ready to raise a family of four on just $8.50 an hour, so we knew we were going to have to do without certain things. We just never dreamed those things would be food and our car.

We had a brand new Subaru Wagon, perfect for a family with a dog. It did not look like those bulky boats back in the day. It was quite sporty—with room for the kids, groceries and our dog, Sara. About six months after purchasing the car, my husband felt convinced we needed to get out of debt, and the only debt we had was that car. Up for sale it went! I relished the time we had the car while waiting for a buyer, because the only other car we had was my husband's little Volkswagen Rabbit. There were no calls for about three months, so I began to wonder if this was what God wanted. Of course it was, but I could not understand why He would want us to have only one car when I had two girls in sports and summer was upon us. During the summers we were rarely home because of the tennis camps and intense gymnastics training as the team was getting ready for their season to begin in the fall.

I remember it like it was yesterday. I know that is a cliché, but so true. It was the month of May, and we got a phone call from someone interested in buying the car. He came over that evening, and agreed to purchase the car. As my husband was drawing up the papers, I could not even be in the same room. I was sitting on the floor in our bedroom, in the dark, with my knees pulled into my chest crying—my freedom was being sold in the other room. In that moment I heard the voice of God so clearly it was almost audible. He said, "*I* will take care of you. I *will* take care of you. I will *take care* of you!"

A few weeks went by after the sale of the car, and I got a phone call from my brother. Apparently he had been involved in an illegal situation, landing him in jail for a few weeks. The reason for the phone call was that he wanted me to take care of his truck while he was doing his time. It was difficult to show sadness for him doing jail time, when I was so excited to have my own car again. It was only a few weeks, but I would take it. It was a beat up truck with a blotchy paint job, but I did not care.

Just before my brother got out of jail, my girlfriend was over for a visit and told me she was headed for Hungary on a mission trip, and would I be willing to take her car for the month she was going to be gone? Of course I would!

I was elated about having my own transportation, but it was quickly erased as I stood in the kitchen the next morning and looked at all my empty cupboards, along with my barren refrigerator shelves. I stood there looking at emptiness. I had no food to feed my family. The girls had gotten scholarships so we did not have to pay for their sports, our bills were paid, we even had a car, but the empty cupboards still screamed at me. As my knees buckled to the kitchen floor, I began to cry out to God, "How am I going to feed my family?" Within a few moments there was a knock at the door. It was the godparents of my oldest daughter. When I opened the door they asked me to come outside. They explained they had just been to Costco, one of those big warehouse stores where people buy items in bulk, and they had bought way too much. Would we be willing to take some of the stuff off their hands? After they brought some of the food in, they simply bid me good day, and left. As they pulled away, my mom pulled in the driveway. She had a trunk load of food. She proceeded to explain that she just cleaned out her big freezer from the garage and had way too much, so she brought it to us. Within the hour, my cupboards and refrigerator were full.

The rest of that summer, people kept asking us if they could keep their car at our home while they were on vacation. One day I walked outside and we had four cars in our driveway, and none of them were ours! God kept His word. He took care of me and my family. He showed me throughout the summer that He is not only faithful, but creative. He cared that my girls loved their sports, and He made a way to get them there. He even made it fun by being able to drive different cars for the whole summer.

PROVISION IN THE MIDST OF THE DELAY

When Joshua and Caleb spied out the Promised Land[4] they **saw** God's provision—the grape clusters so huge that it took two men using a pole to carry them. They had faith for God's provision, but because of the disobedience of the other ten spies, and subsequently the Israelites, they were *delayed* from getting into the Promised Land at that time. Even so, God was still faithful and provided for them until the time came to enter into the Promised Land. If they had been angry and bitter, it would have disqualified them from entering into the Promised Land for the second time. They needed to let disappointment go, and continue to trust God that He is not only *able*, but *willing* to provide in the midst of the *delay*. Caleb was so in tune with the pledge that God gave him that even at

83

eighty years old he could still take the mountain territory of his promise.

The same was true for Joseph when he was in jail right before he was about to be promoted.[5] He helped the king's baker and the cupbearer. He asked them to remember him and to help him get out of jail. The cupbearer told him he would remember him, but then forgot about him for two full years. This delay must have been extremely tough. He probably saw the cupbearer as his ticket out of jail, but then the delay hit and he felt forgotten. Be on guard that your delay does not bring a spirit of discouragement. The opportunity for discouragement that Joseph faced would have been incredible. Satan was offering a banner of betrayal over him—not only by the cupbearer and Potiphar's wife, but also by his own family members. True to Joseph's *developed character*, he came to believe that God had the best for him.

> Be on guard that your delay does not bring a spirit of discouragement.

When we truly believe that God has the best for us and also "has our back," then it does not matter what people say or do. Yes it still hurts, but we know that God will turn it around for good, because He truly loves us. That is an extremely tough lesson to learn, and one that takes a great deal of time. Joseph said it best when he told his brothers, "As for you, you meant evil against me, *but* God meant it for good in order to bring about this present result."[6] God will turn around any delay to bring a good result. God's delays are not necessarily delays at all, *but* scheduled appointed times that we need to show up for.

God can use anyone or anything for our provision, so stay open to what He will send our way even if it is held up or delayed. The Bible says, "Your Father knows exactly what you need before you ask Him!"[7] Do not fall into the trap of thinking, "Well, that cannot be God because He would not do it *this* way." If He can cause bread (manna) to literally rain from the skies, then He can use any means necessary to get us the provision that is coming. Below is a story of God's healing in the midst of delay.

CHRISTINA'S STORY

I want to thank God for my life. At birth I was declared clinically dead. I was diagnosed with cerebral palsy at two years old. The doctors told my parents that I would never succeed or have a productive life. The doctors also said that I would never have children. I wore braces on my legs until the fourth grade, and because of it went through terrible pain both physically and emotionally. God has brought me through some miraculous events and situations since then.

As a result of God's power and love, I have survived, thrived, and overcome. I am learning to walk again. I have two sons that are my blessings and are miracles. God manifested healing in my body this year! He touched me with His ongoing, miraculous power and fifty-two years of nerve pain is gone... and I am beginning to take steps without a walker!

I want to thank Jesus Christ, for all He is, does, and gives! I thank God for my family and friends that support me, and I want to give God all the glory! He has given me so much love. Truly, He is a miracle working God! My heart, love, and prayers go out to you in your own Wilderness experience.

One of my favorite quotes is, "When in need—intercede!"

PROVISION WHEN YOU HAVE NOTHING LEFT

When there was a drought in the land, God told Elijah to go to a widow who would provide for him. He was probably expecting a rich, wealthy widow who had more than enough to share. But what he got was a poor widow who had nothing left. Imagine his disappointment when he met her. When Elijah saw her, he asked her for a cup of water. No problem for her with that one. Off she went to get it for him, but then he asked for some bread. At this request she replied that she had only enough flour and oil to make one meal with her son, and then expected to die. Elijah asked her to give him some of her bread first. I would have felt bad asking any lady (no less a widow) to give up her last meal. Our provision comes from obedience. Sometimes our obedience is in *asking,* and sometimes it is in *giving.* Elijah was obedient to God by *asking* her for her last meal, and the widow was obedient by *giving* Elijah what he requested. When Elijah asked the widow for her bread he was causing her to release her faith. When the widow gave Elijah her bread, the bread and oil was multiplied. They all had enough to last them the entire time through the drought. She had given all that she had, and God multiplied it and sustained her, her son, and Elijah throughout the entire famine!

> **Our provision comes from obedience. Sometimes our obedience is in asking, and sometimes it is in giving.**

It is one thing when God asks us for something that we have more than enough of (like the water for the widow), but it is quite another when He asks us for the very *last* thing we have. There may be a time in the Wilderness when God will ask us for the very last thing we have in order to test our heart and see if we will believe Him at His word. By giving it to Him, we are releasing our faith for His provision. His ways are definitely not our ways.

Gary Keesee, a pastor and businessman, once said, "When we give God our offering, it changes Kingdoms. It goes out of our hand from the world system (or kingdom) and it gets placed into God's hands (or into His Kingdom), and then He is able to multiply it." Here is an exemplary story of this very concept.

JACQUELIN'S STORY

When I was pregnant with my first child, I quit work during my second month, not because I needed to, but because we discovered that a young single father and his four year old son needed a place to live. The father had accepted Christ a few months before and was trying desperately to find a new safe and affordable place for himself and his little boy to live. He knew he needed to get away from the bad influence of his old drinking and drug using buddies and move forward in his new life. We had a four bedroom home, sparsely furnished, but we had the room. We took them in for free during the remaining seven months of my pregnancy so he could work and save money toward his own place. That little boy never had a mother. This is why I quit work. I decided to spend time with him and care for him as if he were my own. We knew this would provide a great head start for them both. The dad also learned parenting skills which would benefit him later when they would be on their own.

That financial sacrifice of quitting work early left us with little money toward meeting needs for our new baby. When my daughter was born, she weighed almost ten pounds, and many of the infant clothes we had been given did not fit her at birth. I was able to exchange some things, but by the time she was three months old I had no clothes for her. We had decided that I would continue to stay home, so money was tight. My husband was in sales and worked on commission, so believe me, money was *tight*!

I stood in the hallway one day and said, "Lord, you see the need, my baby is in diapers with only two t-shirts and I am wrapping her in blankets to keep her warm, and there are no clothes and no money for new clothes. I am going to stand here in this hallway and seek You until You tell me what to do. I obeyed You months ago to help meet the needs of two other people, now I need You to meet *my* need for my baby." I stood there so long hearing nothing. I began to think "Uh, oh, I wonder if I will be standing in this hallway the better part of the day," but I had stuck my neck out and told God I would wait on Him right there where I stood.

Suddenly it came to my heart, "Give away all the clothes you have not worn in the last year." I was stunned, because that would be well over half my closet. New things I had bought right before getting pregnant, (cute things because I had not been planning on getting pregnant), plus various sizes throughout the pregnancy, and then all my maternity clothes, and of course pretty dressy outfits, business suits from work, etc. They were such nice things that the place I donated them to called me back and asked me if I had made a mistake! I assured them no.

It was interesting that when I had an immediate need, the first thing God did was have me *give*, and *give abundantly*! I asked Him "Okay, of course I will do what You tell me, but HOW is this going to cover my need for my three month old baby girl?" Silence.

Two days later I got a phone call from a friend I had just made at a mommy's babysitting co-op. She was fun to be around. She had three children, and her youngest was a little girl who was about eighteen months old and tiny for her age. Karen asked me cautiously, "Would you be comfortable with me offering you my little Natalie's clothes? Some new mothers only want new clothes for their baby, but Natalie has such beautiful things from her grandmas. I have a year's worth of clothing here, plus I have the beautiful items from her sister as well." I told her, "Come on over, I am so pleased you thought of me."

I thought she would show up with a small box of items, but instead she showed up with three full sized thirty-three gallon plastic bags *full* of top-of-the-line baby and toddler clothes... plus older toddler clothes ... *and* shoes, coats, hats, and dressy dresses! It took me a full day to sort through it all, and I was able to give away out of what I received. She asked me if I could continue to use anything, whenever she had items her little girls had outgrown, I would get first choice!

There was such a continuous abundance of clothes provided over the *next five years*, I never had to shop for my daughter at all, year round—all her needs continued to be met! Truly, God supplied exceedingly, abundantly beyond what I could think or ask when I turned to Him, obeyed, and trusted.

MEET OUR EVERY NEED

God can truly meet our every need whether it is totally by the hand of others, or if we have a part to play in the process. We need to be obedient to what He tells us to do, even if it makes absolutely no sense. His provision is always on time, even through the delays. His timing is impeccable, even though at times, we may not understand. He is always faithful and has gone before our journey to provide along the way. He will meet our every need.

OUR PRAYER TO GOD

God,

You are the God of More-Than-Enough. Thank you that Your provisions are new every morning and great is Your faithfulness. I will praise You and thank You each day for my provision, whether it looks great or small. You can meet my needs and even surpass them in any way You choose. I will be completely obedient to give to anyone or any place that you tell me to. I know that as I give it to You, that it changes Kingdoms—where you can bless it and multiply it.

I will continue to believe even in the midst of the delays, because you are never late, but always on time. I ask for the wisdom to be a good steward of what is in my hand. I pray that you multiply it as I offer it up to you with an open hand. I am generous with my finances, time, and talent. I am a generous giver with all that You have given me. Thank You for Your provision. May I never despise the days of manna, but I completely trust that You are the God of More-Than-Enough!

Amen

GOD'S PRAYER TO US

My Child,

I am the Lord your provider, and I give good gifts to my children. Do not fret or worry about what you shall eat or what you shall wear. I have truly clothed the lilies of the field and look how radiant they are. You are more beautiful than the lilies, and I will call out that beauty in you because you need to shine. Your light shines in a big way. Trust me for your provision.

There may be no grapes on the vine, nor cattle in the stalls, yet I am still your Provider and it will come in due season if you patiently wait for it with expectancy. For My ways are not your ways. Even in those times when you feel like I have let you down, I have still been your Provider. For My name is Jehovah-Jireh— The Lord Who Provides. My very name is who I AM.

You will begin to see that I was there all along. I will show you how I was there in the latter rain. Trust Me to provide for you. Praise Me with what you have. Praise Me in the dance. Praise Me no matter what the circumstances around you may look like, for I do not change, and I will take care of you through any drought you may face. I will never leave you nor forsake you, and I will always care for those whom I love. And I loved you enough to give you the best that I had!

Love,
Jehovah Jireh
The Lord Will Provide

STUDY GUIDE

1. What is God asking you to do that may be taking you out of your comfort zone? Obedience is better than sacrifice. Obedience is the key in journeying out of the Wilderness. Commit to writing it down in your journal, and doing it this week even if you do not know why.

2. What has been delayed in the Wilderness? Release that thing to God. In prayer, ask God to break off a spirit of discouragement or depression (or any other negative emotion), that may have come upon you in the Wilderness. Write down in your journal what you feel like God is telling you about that situation.

3. Tell a trusted friend this week one of your favorite God Stories of how the Lord came through for you. Write it down and post it on your bulletin board, or put it on your electronic device as a reminder of how God provided. It will be a faith builder.

ENDNOTES

1. Exodus 3:21-22 (NASB, Emphasis added).
2. Jeremiah 31:17 (NASB).
3. 1 Samuel 25.
4. Numbers 13.
5. Genesis 40.
6. Genesis 50:20a (NASB).
7. Matthew 6:8b (NLT).

CHAPTER FIVE

PROVISION IN THE WILDERNESS

PART 2

"Our barns will be filled with every kind of provision. Our sheep will increase by thousands, by tens of thousands in our fields."
Psalm 144:13 (NIV)

ncouragement is always a precious commodity in the Wilderness. It is as important as water is in the desert. We should never underestimate the power of encouragement in our story. In the Bible it says, "They overcame him (*the devil*) because of the blood of the Lamb and because of the word of *their testimony*."[1] By sharing our *God Stories* with those around us, it will encourage them to make it through and enter their Promised Land. It becomes a double blessing because we are encouraging ourselves too, as we call to remembrance the things He has done for us. "He who refreshes others will himself be refreshed."[2]

There are countless stories of God's provision. In this chapter we will continue to recount some awesome *God Stories* to bring hope and encouragement through this Wilderness season.

PROVISION IN THE MIDST OF LOSS

In the Bible, God sustained the widow's family and Elijah through the drought, but later the widow's son got sick and died. She must have been angry and grieving. She gave it all up, and then her son got sick and died. In response, Elijah cried out to God and prayed over the boy three times and he was resurrected. The Wilderness is the time between the death and resurrection of a dream or destiny. The first time the widow *thought* she and her son would die, but they did not.

> The Wilderness is the time between the death and resurrection of a dream or destiny.

Fear seized her the *first* time about what *may (could possibly)* happen, but God came through. The second time she had to deal with something else. No longer a potential threat, her son's death became a reality. Was she going to trust Him now, when her son actually *did* die? It required two different levels of faith. Her response to her son's resurrection was interesting. She said, "*Now I know for sure* that you are a man of God, and that the Lord truly speaks through you."[3] Was she not sure before when God provided food for her family through the entire drought?

It is one level of faith to stand and believe through the *fear*. It requires an entirely different level of faith to believe in a God who resurrects dead things. Believing God to resurrect a marriage, a house, finances, or wayward children takes a whole new level of faith. Resurrection faith has power. Paul talks about knowing the *dynamis* (Greek) power of the resurrection in the book of Philippians. It goes back to the Word that the Lord gave me when He said, "Now let death become life. Let death be as nothing in light of resurrection power." Do we trust Him to resurrect things that are "gone" in our lives?

Sometimes I imagine what the disciples thought after Jesus died. He tried to warn them, but I do not think they really understood the fact that He was going to die. When He died on the cross, they all scattered in a multitude of directions. Some decided to go back into their previous professions, but God brought them all back together in the upper room and gave them the Holy Spirit and the *dynamis* power of the resurrection.

It is through the death of something in our lives—whether it is a dream, hopes, marriage, or our finances, that we have the opportunity to see the power of God resurrecting that thing. The experience cements an immovable faith in us that last a lifetime. We will never again be shaken to the very core of *who* we are, because we know *who* God is. Below is a story of when everything seems "gone," God is faithful to provide.

DEBBIE'S STORY

We were beginning divorce proceedings. My now ex-husband was ordered by the court to leave the premises of our residence. Since no one was home, I agreed that it would be alright for him to come take what he needed. When I returned that evening, I opened the door and my heart sank. My breath left me. My five year old son cried out, "Mommy, we have been robbed!" Carrying my little girl, I knelt down to comfort him, fighting back my tears. Internally, I was seeking God for the courage for what was to come out of my mouth. "Oh, honey, no. It is all at daddy's house now. That way when you visit him you will have your bed, and our other things and it will be familiar to you. God is with us, my love." We borrowed some blankets and slept on the floor that night.

The next morning, I went to the business I was helping to start. I pressed forward and did not talk about it with my associates. We received a phone call. Our large initial wire and cable inventory order had been shipped two weeks early, and our new warehouse still had occupants that would not be vacated until the end of the month. My boss tossed me the keys and said, "You have to fix it, Deb." I was on my way.

In the truck, my eyes filled with tears. "So, how are we going to handle this one, Lord? In You I can do all things... right?" In only a few weeks, the company I worked for was taken over and we all lost our jobs. I was in an accident that totaled my car. My landlord (who was our neighbor and like a grandmother to my kids) died. We had just received a thirty day notice to move. I was going through a rough divorce and raising two children on my own. I lost my friends and relationships with my family. We had lost all our furniture. We had no money, and now no place for this huge load of copper that would be here tomorrow. "Lord, please give me favor with these people. I do not see a way, but I know You do. My heart is so heavy, please help me." Wiping my blurred watery eyes, only my subconscious noticed the *Furniture Liquidation* sign as I pulled into the parking lot.

As I walked into what was to be our new office, I was greeted by the sweetest, most overdue pregnant woman I had ever seen! I listened as she told the story of her family business, and how it was now time for her to raise her family. I could not have been happier for her. Her story brought me joy. Then, I explained our "premature delivery" predicament

101

and she invited me to the warehouse, to see if there was room for the reels. As she opened the huge doors, she said, "Do you know anyone who may need some furniture?" I tried to speak, but only a half laugh, half cry, noise blurted out. She had opened the doors to the most breathtaking furniture anyone could ever dream of owning. Her company supplied Orange County California model homes. Struggling to cap my emotions, I explained to her a portion of what had just happened at home.

She stopped the men that were working, asked them to clear a truck, and started loading it for me! Huge elevated beds with pillow top mattresses, luxurious sofas, marble tables, hand-painted room dividers, gorgeous beveled framed mirrors, a lovely dining room table. Enough furniture for the whole house ... for free! They even moved it all in and put it together for me. My little ones were thrilled with amazement when they saw what God had done for us. God restored our home with furniture that was better than we could ever have asked or imagined. It also made room in the warehouse for the load of copper that was delivered the next day. I am forever grateful and confident of His faithfulness. It was God.

> God restored our home ... better than we could ever have asked or imagined.

No doubt about it. Over ten years later, all that He has built in us and strengthened us is undeniable.

YOUR PROVISION DIFFERENT THAN EXPECTED— GET "THE UPDATE"

There is a constant need to check in with God and get "The Update." Many times we get an initial direction from the Lord and then charge off. We think that Word will carry us through all the different seasons. But sometimes a Word of provision is only for *one* season, and we need to get "*The Update*" and possibly move in a different direction. It is not that we heard incorrectly from the Lord, but our lives and circumstances are being transformed as we continue on in the Wilderness. Maybe He needed to give us only a partial Word at the beginning (even though we thought it was the full Word), because He knew we could not handle the big picture at that particular time. He may give us pieces at a time, like bread crumbs leading us to our Promised Land.

David is an exemplary example of getting "The Update." Every time he went into battle, he inquired of the Lord *IF* he was to go into battle and *HOW* he was to fight. These are two fundamental questions we can ask the Lord. "Is this where you want me to go? And how do you want me to proceed in this situation?" David did not assume that God wanted him to fight in each battle. He first went to the Lord and asked Him if he was to fight. Then he would ask Him for the strategy in the battle. He could have easily rested on his laurels and kept fighting the same way every time, but that would have meant that he would have carried a sling shot with him into every battle. As David grew, both physically and in character, he changed his methods of warfare. He grew to the point where he could go to Ahimelech, the priest in Nob, and ask for Goliath's sword. He was older and could now handle a sword of that caliber, whereas in his youth he could not. This is the same for Saul's armor. David tried to wear it, but it was just too big and he was not accustomed to fighting with that kind of armor. Later in battle, when he was older, David could use heavier armor because he had gained physical strength.

The key is to have self-awareness of what we can handle, and to know where we are with the Lord at the time of the

> **The key is to have self-awareness of what we can handle, and to know where we are with the Lord at the time of the battle.**

battle. Take what we know to be true. Take the level of faith that we carry at the time. Take the level of forgiveness that we have and lay it at His feet, then the level of armor (or what we can handle) will grow. As we progress, God will give us more challenging problems to solve. So always get "The Update." Never assume that just because something worked in the past, it will be the same next time around. Each time is different. This causes us to look to the Lord and to be fully reliant on Him. It is based on a *relationship* with the Lord, and not some magic formula that gives the one-two knock out punch to the devil. Below is a story of how God gave a couple "The Update" when they wanted to buy their first home.

SANDRA'S STORY

We had been renting our current home in Norwalk, California for thirteen years. For many of those years we often dreamed of owning our own home, but we never made enough money for the dream to be a reality. There were a few times during those years where we would drive around to open houses or look on the internet for something in our price range. The only available homes were condos, located in unsafe neighborhoods, or in Tennessee. There was even a time where my husband had a temporary lapse (forgetting about the calling on our life), and was ready to move to Tennessee, envisioning a simpler life with more for our money. So many were leaving the state at that time, but we knew in our hearts God had us where we were for a reason.

It all began one morning with a phone call from a mom who's son went to the same tennis academy as our daughter. At that time my husband worked in the Corian countertop business, and would take side jobs to make ends meet. She wanted him to come out and give her a quote on a kitchen counter top. We also found out that she was a realtor, and we expressed to her how we would like to own our own home one day. She took it upon herself to begin looking for us, because as a realtor she could see things that were not always advertised on the internet. We were looking for a fixer-upper. We knew they cost less, and we were pretty handy. Plus it would be fun fixing up our own home.

I would meet her first to look at homes, before taking my husband. After a few times I started noticing that she kept showing me condos. I reminded her that we wanted a house, and we had a dog so we really wanted a yard for our dog. Her response was that in this market, we were not going to find a house. She recommended that we settle for a condo, or move to Tennessee. After seeing God's provision over the past thirteen years, this was not acceptable. I expressed to her that God wanted us to have a house, and He would provide one. We did not need to settle for less. As we parted ways, I could see that she was not convinced we were going to be able to purchase a house in Southern California, but it did not matter. I knew God had a house for us. Maybe not now, but it was coming.

A few weeks after that conversation with the realtor, my husband and I once again ventured out on our own driving around and praying to see where God wanted us to live. We headed south, because we always seemed to be going that way for my husband's work and our daughters' activities. As we drove around East Long Beach, there were a lot of homes for sale. It was the height of the housing market where people were outbidding one another for homes. Homes were selling the day they went on the market. But we had a dream, and it was fun to drive around and dream that one day we too would have our own home.

Driving down Wardlow Street, we liked the tree-lined street and the cute homes. When I saw a home with a "For Sale" sign up, I called and got the price of the home. This home was a little different, because the owner was selling it himself with help from an escrow company. We pulled up in front of the house to get the number off the sign. As I was calling the number, my husband said, "There is no way we can afford this house." Just as those words came out of his mouth, I got an answering machine and the recording said, "For God so loved the world that He gave His only begotten Son, so that the world could have everlasting life." I let him listen in on the recording, and just then someone picked up the phone. We explained that we were calling about the house and were wondering if we could see it. They happened to be home, and we happened to be right outside. The home had been on the market for two days. As we walked through the door to this home, the first thing we noticed was that it needed a lot of work. But we were okay with that. As long as the plumbing was copper, we could handle the rest. We did not really care for the floor plan, but could see it had potential. It was a three bedroom, two bathroom home. We would have one more bathroom, and about 400 more square feet than we currently had, and would be closer to everywhere we went. We then asked the price, thanked them for their time and went home.

It was out of our price range. We were pre-qualified and had a $20,000 down payment, but again, it was too expensive. We decided the timing was not right yet, and we would continue to wait. But we needed to get "The Update."

That night, I was up all night arguing with the Lord. It began when He told me to make an offer on the house. I tried to explain that in this market, nobody was going to take less money than they were asking, because they always got more than what they were asking. People were out-bidding one another. He did not seem to understand, not only was the house out of our price range, but it was probably going to sell for more than what they were asking. However, the Lord would not relent, and kept telling me to make an offer. As 6:00 a.m. approached, my husband opened his eyes, and looked right into mine and said, "What?" He knew something was up. I told him that God said to make an offer and what that offer was supposed to be. He did not say anything, got up and went to work. We already resolved that we were going to stay in our rented home, so why was God telling us to make an offer? We did not speak of it again for the next few days, and then my husband phoned me from work and said to make the offer.

I was a bit nervous making that phone call. If they said, "No," we were right where we began, but if we never did anything, we would never know. I made the call and did not get into any details, even though I knew they were Christians. I simply made the offer, and he immediately said, "Yes!" We made an appointment to sign the papers that Saturday. We moved in on June sixteenth. While we were waiting for escrow to close, we got to know the couple we were buying the home from very well. Right after he accepted our offer, he had a lady who wanted the home and was willing to pay $100,000 more than what we offered. But the owner expressed to her that he could not go back on his word to us, because he had to answer to God if he did. We were able to pray with them several times before we moved in. They even let us move our stuff into the garage before escrow closed. They moved out of the country so we never saw them again. God continues to be faithful. We have learned over the course of those thirteen years to never doubt God. If He says He is going to do something, He is going to do it. He is way more creative than we are!

PROVISION IN THE MIDST OF OUR ENEMIES

God can send provision in the *midst* of our enemies or sometimes even by the very *hand* of our enemies. The Bible says, "You prepare a table before me in the presence of my enemies. You anoint my head with oil; my cup overflows. Surely goodness and love will follow me all the days of my life, and I will dwell in the house of the Lord forever."[4]

God can get the provision to us in a multitude of ways, and they are not always the way we expect. It can even be by the very hand of those who have set their course against ours. Here is an encouraging story that illustrates this point.

ERIN'S STORY

I was in a difficult marriage (my husband was not saved), but being a Christian I hung in there until the end. The only lifeline I had was God. When the marriage ended, I began a faith walk that I had never known before. My ex-husband dragged me through the mud, and needless to say, tried everything in the book to have my children taken away from me. We lived in a place where I had no friends or family, and we were surrounded by *his* family and friends. The only place I knew I could go was to my mother's home located in the next state. Through this process, I hung onto the Lord, and He was faithful to guide me the whole way. Miraculously, with permission from the court, I was allowed to move myself and the children to my mother's house temporarily until a decision concerning custody of the children was made. We went through numerous court hearings, and an evaluation process in which the evaluator picked me apart. It was then decided that we would share custody. The children would have to go back and forth between homes. The arrangement was two weeks with him, and then two weeks with me. We knew this was not going to last because two of our children would be starting kindergarten soon.

We knew that once they began school, we would have to fight for who was going to get full custody of the children. After two years of this battle, and with our last mediation to go, the mediator let us know that he could not make this decision. To him we both seemed fit to have full custody. He then ordered another evaluation, and said that the judge would have to decide. He told us that the only thing stopping us from being able to co-parent with each other was the fact that we lived in different states.

I was not able to move back to his state, and my ex-husband was adamant about not moving to the state where I was living. On my way home from mediation that day (it was about a five hour drive) the Lord ministered to my heart. He spoke words of peace that I could not deny. He softly spoke to me and said, "Give him the kids." I replied, "What?" He repeated it to me four times, "Let him have the kids." I knew it was the Lord speaking to my heart. No other could speak to my heart like that. I cried the whole way home, but I did not act on it right away. I still needed to be sure it was the Lord. My sisters in Christ supported me, but also wanted me to make sure it was the Lord. I still knew it was. I slept on it, and sure enough the next day the tugging on my heart persisted, but I still had not acted upon it. I thought, "There is church tonight. Let me see if this is really the Lord telling me to do this. Then I will know for sure."

Sure enough, not even half way through the worship service, the Spirit filled me and ministered to my heart. I was certain this was something I needed to act upon. Suddenly I had peace, and I was comforted by His Spirit. No sooner was I pulling out of the parking lot to leave service, when my ex-husband called. I told him right then and there. I let him know that I was not going to fight over our children, and that God told me to let him have the kids. He was very surprised and shocked, but happy. He asked why, and I told him again that God told me to let him have the children, and that is why I was doing it. He asked me to move back to his state, and I told him that the Lord did not tell me to move, but to only give him the kids. We ended the conversation. That was one of the hardest things I have ever had to do, but I knew that God was in it. Not more than two hours later he called me back and said, "Well what do you think if I tried it out there, and moved out where you are? If it does not work, I will move back and take the children with me." I told him, "That is your decision to make. I have already given you everything that I have to give (our children)." The Lord kept telling me to keep the ball in his court and not to pick it up again.

> **The Lord kept telling me to keep the ball in his court and not to pick it up again.**

Two days later my ex-husband called me again and said, "I just want to let you know that I do not want to do this without you. The boys need their mother. I am looking to see if there are any jobs or possibilities of me moving there. I am not sure yet, but I am looking into it." I got a little excited and thought to myself, "Well if God has anything to with this, which I know He does, than you will have no problem finding a job!" I still did not get too excited, but I knew God was working. A week later I got a phone call and it was him. He told me that his friend was able to get him a job and he was trying to find a place to live so he could move to the state where I was living. I was praising the Lord. I was holding my breath, because he had not moved yet. Not more than a month later, he was fully moved in. Now this man who I had been fighting with, and who once sought after everything I had, is now a friend and we invite each other to coffee.

The Bible says in Proverbs 16:7, "When people's lives please the Lord, even their enemies are at peace with him." My story is proof that this Word is true!

WHAT IS IN YOUR HAND?

There is a story in the Bible of a widow who came to Elisha and asked him how she could pay off her debt. Elisha asked her, "What is in your hand?" She said, "Some oil." He told her to borrow as many pots (or containers) that she could find from her neighbors. So she asked her boys to help her get some pots from those around her. After she collected them, Elisha told her to start pouring the oil into the containers. She did this and the oil continued to come out until she reached the end of the last container.[5]

God's provision for the widow came from what was in her *hand* AND what was in her *heart*. What was in her *hand* was the *oil* that she had in her house. What was in her *heart* was the *faith* that she had for the amount of pots that

God's provision for the widow came from what was in her hand AND what was in her heart.

she collected. The amount of her pots set the level of her faith. Her "provision was in direct proportion to her faith and ability to receive."[6] If she had faith for more jars, then she could have gone out to neighbors that were further away to get more.

There is another story in the Bible that illustrates this point. Elisha was talking to one of the kings about a battle the king was going to fight. Elisha told him to shoot an arrow out the window as an act of faith that signified that the king would win the battle. The king did this act and shot the arrow out of the window. Then Elisha asked the king to do another act of faith to represent his *complete* victory against the enemy. Elisha said, "Now pick up the other arrows and strike them against the ground. So the king picked them up and struck the ground three times. But the man of God was angry with him. You should have struck the ground five or six times! He exclaimed. Then you would have beaten Aram until it was entirely destroyed. Now you will be victorious only three times."[7] The king's provision was in direct correlation to his faith. He struck the ground only three times. This limited his victory to only three battles. The king's faith (represented through striking the ground) set the level of his blessing in his kingdom.

How many times have we limited God in His provision for us by limiting our own faith? The time in the Wilderness is a chance to expand our faith to believe for bigger things than we have ever believed before. As we are expanded, our ability to receive all that God has for us is expanded as well.

One time I received a picture from the Lord of provisions coming to me in different ways. The last picture I saw was the final provision coming on a *conveyor belt*. I felt God speak to my heart and say, "Pay attention to the *conveyor belt!*" I realized that the provision is important, but it is equally important to set up the systems in place to handle the provision that is coming.

When Joseph became second in command to Pharaoh, Joseph built storehouses to contain all the grain that was coming in. In addition to the storehouses, he created a system to give it away in due season during the drought.[8] Jesus fed 5,000 men with the five loaves and two fish. He used baskets to collect the leftovers.[9] He did not want any of God's provision to go to waste. It is imperative that we put systems in place to handle our provision, and to be good stewards of what God *has* and *will* entrust to us.

The important thing right now is to be wise with what God has entrusted to us during the Wilderness time. We may feel like we have nothing, but the widow with the jar of oil only had a "jar of oil" (not much). But God used it and multiplied it according to her faith.

I have a friend who is a single mother and she is constantly giving. God is incredible in His absolute *Father's heart* in providing for her. I have never seen such *out of the ordinary* provision for someone; *however,* I have never seen such *sacrificial giving.* She is a single mom that gives everything down to her last penny, even her kitchen table in a yard sale to send her teenage children on mission trips. God has always provided for her. She never gives out of her surplus, but always out of her need. It reminds me of the churches of Macedonia who gave out of their need. "They are being tested by many troubles, and they are very poor. But they are also filled with abundant joy, which has overflowed in rich generosity. For I (*Paul*) can testify that they gave not only what they could afford, but far more. And they did it of their own free will."[10]

God's hand is not too short that He cannot provide for us. But sometimes His provisions come as we reach out a helping hand to those around us. If we give, even from our lack, then we are showing God truly how much we trust Him to take care of us and our need. The challenge is to do something out of the ordinary in giving, whether it is giving of our time or finances. As we step out and stretch in this area of giving and become more generous, we will begin to see God's provision manifest in a multitude of ways.

OUR PRAYER TO GOD

God,

Thank You that You are the God of the Angel-Armies, and my God who provides. You are faithful and Your Word is true. You are not a man that you should lie, nor the son of man that you change your mind. Do You speak and then not act? Do You promise and not fulfill?

For Your ways are bigger than anything I could ever come up with on my own. One creative idea from You alone could provide for a lifetime—just like You did with the woman that collected the pots. I pray for creative ideas and witty inventions, because

You are a God of creative miracles. I pray You will show me how to partner with You for my provision, and I will be 100% obedient to what You are calling me to do even if it makes no sense. I will collect the "pots" even if I do not understand. Thank You for Your provision, for it may be brilliantly disguised in impossible situations, because You are the God of impossibilities!

Amen

GOD'S PRAYER TO US

My Child,

I have entrusted you with much. You may feel like it is little, but it is much in My kingdom. Remember the story of the widow giving all that she had? That was the story I remember. That was the story that I recounted in My Word. Do not despise the days of small beginnings. This is where My greatest work is being accomplished. This is where I move and build you into the person I created you to be. Live life with an outstretched arm; an open hand to those around you who are in need, and watch Me work in amazing ways. I will take notice. I will take care of you. Stand fast in the fact that I will provide and will not leave you, nor forsake you. You are my beloved and my banner over you is love. What good earthly father does not take good care of His children? How much more will I take good care of you and give you good gifts? I will provide for you and I will always give you exactly what you need in this Wilderness season.

Love,
Jehovah Jireh
The Lord Will Provide

STUDY GUIDE

1. Read the story of the widow found in 2 Kings 4 and ask God what is in your hand? What are you to do with what is in your hand? Write your answers in your journal.

2. During your prayer time, ask the Lord to help you put systems in place to be a good steward of what He has already given you, and what He is going to entrust you with. For example, if it is finances, then possibly create a budget. If it is time, then set a certain aside for devotions or serving in a ministry.

3. Ask a trusted friend this week to tell you one of their favorite God Stories of how the Lord came through for them. Encourage them to write it down for both of you, so that it will be a faith builder.

ENDNOTES

1. Revelation 12:11a (NASB, Emphasis added).
2. Proverbs 11:25b (NIV).
3. I Kings 17:24b (NLT, Emphasis added).
4. Psalm 23:5-6 (NIV).
5. 2 Kings 4:1-7.
6. Spirit-Filled Bible. Footnote from 2 Kings 4.
7. 2 Kings 13:18-19 (NLT).
8. Genesis 41:25-56.
9. Mark 6:35-43.
10. 2 Corinthians 8:2-3 (NLT, Emphasis added).

CHAPTER SIX

WHY ALL THE COMPLAINING?

*"Now when the people complained,
it displeased the Lord."*
Numbers 11:1a (NKJV)

In Hebrew, the word for Wilderness is *Midbar*. *Midbar* means *uninhabited land*[1] which is what we customarily think about when we hear the word Wilderness. But the most interesting meaning for Midbar is *mouth* (as an organ of speech).[2] A critical part of the Wilderness is our mouth. *What* we speak *about* our circumstances, is just as important as what we *do* in our circumstances.

WHAT WE SPEAK IN THE WILDERNESS

Our mouth is the gatekeeper in the Wilderness. Whether we make it out of the Wilderness or not is in large part based on what we say. Our mouth speaks what our heart believes. What we *say* in the Wilderness is vitally important. "For the *mouth* speaks out of that which fills the heart...I tell you, that every *careless word* that people speak, they shall give an accounting for it in the day of judgment. For by your *words* you will be justified, and by your *words* you will be condemned."[3]

David said, "I pour out my complaint before Him, before Him I tell my trouble."[4] Pouring out our complaint *to God* is different than complaining to others. Many times in the Psalms, David cried out to God and poured out his complaint, but by the end of the Psalm He gave God praise. He always ended by refocusing his words on God and the greatness of God. There will be times we need to go to God and pour out our hearts to Him in full surrender, but at the end we always need to refocus and remember just how great our God is.

Complaining is different than pouring out our hearts to God. Complaining has an audience with many, but pouring out our hearts to God is a conversation with One— the One true God who can actually help us. The attitude of the heart is the key that distinguishes the difference. If we are pouring out our

> **Complaining has an audience with many, but pouring out our hearts to God is a conversation with One.**

hearts to truly get help or find answers, it is different than just complaining in order to whine about something or seek sympathy for our condition.

One day I was at the gym and a woman next to me complained the whole time I was working out. This behavior was typical of other encounters with her, so I offered some advice and got to the root of her complaint. I could tell she did not like this, because in essence I *shut her down* in her complaining. But that was not what she wanted. She wanted the "audience," and for me to pet her complaint. She did not want any solutions, only to whine. Her heart was exposed and she walked away, because I would not give her the "audience" she was looking for.

Complaining and unbelief disqualify us to enter into His promises. Complaining is a *by-product of resentment* for what we are going through. In essence it is telling God that He has no clue about what He is doing, which grieves the Lord. He sees the bigger picture and is at work to accomplish His end game in our lives. Things might not be the way we thought, because His ways are not our ways. The nature and character of God is that He is *good* all the time. That is His divine nature and character. He knows His plans for us and that they are *good*—even when the circumstances seem contrary. Circumstances have a voice. Sometimes it feels like that voice is screaming for us to pay attention to it, when in fact, we need to silence it with *our own* voice. In the Wilderness we will need to press forward *not because* of the circumstances around us, but *in spite of* the circumstances around us.

Peter is a good example of believing God in the face of contrary circumstances that surrounded him. Peter asked Jesus to bid him to come and walk on the water. So Peter stepped out of the boat and took a couple steps, but when he saw the wind and the waves crashing around him, he began to sink. At this point he had a key decision to make: "Do I speak to the circumstances, or do I let the circumstances speak to me?" Peter let the circumstances speak. He called upon Jesus to save him which He did. Once they were back in the boat, Jesus rebuked Peter for his lack of faith. Had he exercised his faith and spoken to his circumstances, he would have walked on water, just like Jesus. It is better to speak to the circumstances in our lives with faith and tell them to line up with the Word of God, than to continually live in fear asking Him to bail us out.

> It is better to speak to circumstances in our lives with faith and tell them to line up with the Word of God, than to continually live in fear asking Him to bail us out.

God will place many of us at this exact juncture in our lives. He will ask us to "get out of the boat." He may ask us to let go of a business deal, leave a particular job, or sell something that is extremely valuable to us. It is at this occasion of getting out of the boat that rocks everything we believe. We may think that things will be great because we stepped out in obedience, but like Peter, we see our tumultuous circumstances and feel more exposed than ever. Maybe Peter thought the wind would die down miraculously when he stepped out of the boat, or that the waves would become like glass. Many times the circumstances do not line up with what *WE* thought they would look like. Everything we have been taught up to that point gets tested. When the circumstances go contrary to what we thought would happen, do we still believe? Do we still trust God? That is the kind of faith God wants to produce in us.

This is the point of being in the Wilderness—to bring out of us the faith that can move mountains. There is no faith when circumstances are not contrary. Faith happens when our beliefs and obedience line up *despite* the circumstances. What we decide at this phase will set the course for our Wilderness journey. Will we go around this mountain one more time, or will we learn the lessons and forge a path through? Our destiny in the Wilderness is all in the power of the tongue, which is a by-product of what our heart really believes. When we choose to speak words of faith to our contrary circumstances, it entrenches our belief as we go deeper with the Lord. The more deep-rooted we become, the more circumstances lose their control over us.

Speaking to our circumstances can be as simple as saying "No!" aloud when a thought enters into our mind that is filled with doubt and worry. One of my friends calls this, "refusing delivery." When something comes to her in the form of a thought or fear, she simply says aloud or in her mind, "I refuse delivery." It is her way of speaking to the circumstance and not allowing that thought to grow in her mind. That is one example of speaking to our circumstances.

WHO'S REPORT?

When the Israelites were getting ready to enter their Promised Land, Moses sent out twelve leaders to spy out the land. Two of the spies, Joshua and Caleb, came back with a good report. The other ten spies gave a bad report. The report of the ten spies said, "We became like grasshoppers in our *own* sight, and *so we were* in their sight."[5] They believed they were grasshoppers, but the truth was that the people in Jericho were scared of *them* and trembling from fear. They had heard the reports of all the plagues

God brought upon Egypt, and how the Lord went before the Israelites to defeat their enemies in the Wilderness. They had been afraid of the Children of Israel for forty years! The Israelites may have *felt* like grasshoppers, but it was not the truth. Even if they did feel like grasshoppers, look how God used the grasshopper (locust) against their enemy in Egypt. Winning the battle is not about the circumstances or how *little* we feel, but realizing how *big* our God is.

Winning the battle is not about the circumstances or how little we feel, but realizing how big our God is.

God struck down the men who gave a bad report to the Children of Israel. "Those men who brought out the very bad report of the land died by a plague before the Lord."[6] The words of our mouth not only impact ourselves, but it impacts those around us as well. People in our family are listening, along with people in our sphere of influence. Which report are we giving every day to those around us and to ourselves? No matter which report we give, it will become true. Joshua and Caleb were the only two spies that eventually entered the Promised Land based on the words of their mouth, and their faith that God would prevail. Our mouth can steer us straight into loss and destruction or straight into our Promised Land—*if* we let it.

God had great patience with the Children of Israel in the Wilderness. They grumbled. They complained. They tested HIM even though the Wilderness was supposed to be about Him testing THEM to see what was in their heart. Even through all that, He was still going to allow them to come into the Promised Land. All God wanted was for them to believe—believe Him and trust Him that He wanted the best for them. Believe Him that He would make a way where there seems to be no way. Believe Him that He is a great and powerful God who sincerely loves them. It is when they, by choice, stubbornly refused to believe God that *they aborted their own destiny* that He had planned for them.

I know someone who wrote a book about how God healed her of cancer. A lady gave it to her friend to read. The next time they met, she asked her friend how she liked the book. The lady said, "I think it is great how the Lord healed the author of the book, but it will not happen to me." By her own utterance she had sealed her fate. It was her own lack of faith and unbelief that limited God's hand to heal her. Even Jesus, when in His own home town, could not do a lot of miracles because of their unbelief. One of the stories in the Bible says, "A man with leprosy came and knelt before him and said, 'Lord if you are willing, you can make me clean.' Jesus reached out His hand and touched the man. "*I am willing*," He said. "Be clean!"[7] Jesus said, "*I am willing.*" He is willing to heal the giant circumstances in our marriages, our finances, or our health. It is a matter of shifting old mindsets and lining up our tongue with what God has spoken about us. It is creating a new mindset that becomes the new wine to put into the new wine skin.

COMPLAINING AND GRUMBLING

Grumbling means "to complain in a surly manner, protest about something, or to mutter in discontent."[8] The medical definition of *murmur* is "an *atypical* sound of the heart, typically indicating a functional or structural abnormality."[9] When we murmur (grumble), it brings to the surface what is really in our hearts as believers. It is *atypical* of what God had planned when He created our hearts. God created us to be thankful, which is the opposite of grumbling. What we believe in our hearts comes out when we murmur or complain. If we are truly trusting God, then murmuring or complaining has no place in our vocabulary. The Scripture says, "My *tongue* (is) the pen of a ready writer."[10] Through the mouth the heart speaks. It writes the script for what we believe God can do.

The Israelites were complaining against Moses and said, "Leave us alone that we may serve the Egyptians. For it would have been better for us to serve the Egyptians than to *die in the*

131

Wilderness."[11] Their mouths were speaking things that were contrary to what God had spoken over them. God led them to the Wilderness as a transitional process, *not* so they would die in the Wilderness. *They* spoke death over themselves and God honored the word of their mouth. They received what they declared. In the Wilderness, our *mouth*—what we *speak* about our circumstances, has *everything* to do with the outcome of our situation. We are under a new covenant of grace, but we are still accountable for what comes out of our mouth.

The Children of Israel progressed from grumbling to quarreling with Moses and Aaron—God's appointed leaders. If left unchecked, our complaining and grumbling will lead to quarreling with those around us. There was a group of men called the Sons of Korah who were originally from the tribe of Levi. The tribe of Levi became the priests who performed the sacrifices. The Sons of Korah grumbled and complained about Moses and Aaron being their leaders in the Wilderness. God told Moses to separate himself from them, and then came down and killed them. This led to the congregation fleeing in fear. Even after that huge judgment from the Lord, the congregation still complained to Moses and Aaron the very next day. When we are in the Wilderness, it is easy to blame others for *seemingly* unpleasant things that are happening to us. We need to be cautious that we do not grumble or quarrel with those around us in the Wilderness. It is easy to blame others, especially when it lands us in the middle of our own Wilderness experience.

When the Children of Israel came out of Egypt they started complaining, but they were still headed to the Promised Land. At what point did they disqualify themselves from entering in? Even after all their mistakes in the Wilderness (the golden calf, complaining, and coming against Moses and Aaron), the one thing that disqualified them was *their mouth*. Their mouth was in agreement with their lack of faith. There is a Scripture that talks about when two are in agreement as touching anything that it will happen.[12] We usually think about this in the "positive" sense as we stand in prayer with someone else for a request that we have. The principle is also true in the "negative" sense, and still carries the same weight of agreement. We can *believe* in our hearts and *confess* with our mouths things that are contrary to what God has promised over our lives.

Do we have internal agreement with the things we are confessing? The Children of Israel did have internal agreement between their belief and what they spoke, but it was from a heart of *unbelief.* They saw the huge fruit of the Promised Land, yet still did not stand in faith that it was theirs to possess. Lack of faith is saying that God is too small to handle the circumstances. God had already proven Himself by all the miracles He did to deliver His people and get them out of Egypt. He parted the Red Sea and gave them manna and quail. God had done so much to *prove* Himself in their lives, and now when faced with another challenge they simply did not believe. Complaining tills the *soil of unbelief* in our lives so that when the time comes to enter in, we walk away in disobedience. On the other hand, a heart of faith will till the *soil of belief,* and when the time comes we will fully walk into our own personal Promised Land.

> Complaining tills the soil of unbelief in our lives so that when the time comes to enter in, we walk away in disobedience.

We have a personal Promised Land that God wants us to inherit and enter. We need to begin setting the stage now for our hearts to have fertile soil to *believe* and *receive* that He will get us through our Wilderness journey. The days when we do not *feel* like entering into His presence, we need to enter in anyway through reading His Word, worship, and prayer. Worship and reading the Word are the keys to unlock the door of our hearts. Prayer facilitates the change that needs to happen to inherit the promises.

THE GRIEVING PROCESS

There are times when we grieve a loss in the Wilderness (sometimes even several losses). It may be the loss of a material possession, the loss of a person, or the loss of an *expectation*. Grieving is an important part of the process in the Wilderness, and everyone will grieve in a different way. It is important to go *through* the grief and not get stuck in it. The Bible says, "Even though I walk *through* the valley of the shadow of death, I will fear no evil, for You are with me; Your rod and Your staff, they comfort me."[13] We walk *through* the valley of the shadow of death. We do not set up camp, make a tent, and wallow in it. We move *through* it.

We may bounce around in different parts of the stages of grief, but we still move through each stage. It does not have to be exactly in sequential order, and we can go back and forth in the different stages until we fully process our grief. The Bible says, "My flesh will...*pitch its tent* and dwell in *hope*."[14] This is where we need to set up our tent—in hope, not in the overwhelming grief of the situation. We need to continue to put something that gives us hope in front ourselves each day. Our journey may be long, and we will need it to encourage us to get to the other side. "Weeping may remain for a night, but rejoicing (joy) comes in the morning."[15] There is an end to the grieving, and God will give us joy.

I have met several Christians who are uncomfortable with grieving. Although they do not outwardly say it, they have what I call a "suck it up mentality." They may mask it in a religious spirit and say, "God has everything under control, so why grieve?" Some may quote "happy" Scriptures to make it all go away. Many of these are good-hearted people that do not know what to do when someone else is grieving. Maybe they have not gone through that particular experience, and therefore cannot really empathize and understand the severity of the situation. Others may be uncomfortable with their own feelings, because they grew up in a home where they were not allowed to express grief. Whatever the case may be, grieving is a natural experience that we all must go through in the Wilderness.

The Bible talks about giving a "sacrifice of praise," and that could not be more true then when we are in the Wilderness. It is genuinely a *sacrifice* of praise. One of the Scriptures I clung to during my grieving time in the Wilderness says, "Why are you cast down, O my inner self? And why should you moan over me and be disquieted within me? Hope in God and wait expectantly for Him, for I shall yet praise Him, Who is the help of my (sad) countenance, and my God."[16] Even in grieving, praising God will give us the power and the strength to continue. It becomes like an energy drink that helps us get through the day.

The best gift to give someone who is grieving in the Wilderness is a non-judgmental, listening ear. Even if it is the same story over and over, that person needs to express their grief over their loss. They do not necessarily need their problems solved (and some are too big to solve anyway), they just need a safe place to vent what they are going through. It is easy to judge what one person has gone through and think it is no big deal, because we are coming from a different set of experiences. That is why it is imperative to have a non-judgmental spirit when listening to them. What may have put one person in the Wilderness, is far different than what has put another person in the Wilderness. The key is to stay open to those who grieve, and be there through their time of pain as best we can.

Grieving is essential and healthy. If we do not grieve at the time of the loss, it will come out in some aspect of our lives later. I have known of people that have not grieved over the death of a loved one until years after they died. Grieving is part of the human experience. Even Jesus experienced grief. The Bible says He was a man of sorrows and familiar with suffering, and He took up our sickness and carried our sorrows (grief).[17] He knows what we are going through and will be there to comfort us in our loss.

Jesus wept and grieved the loss of Lazarus, even when He *knew* He would raise him from the dead and see him that same day. Some of the things we grieve in the Wilderness may be a lost relationship or friendship, the loss of a loved one, loss of a job, loss of a spouse through divorce, or the loss of a home through financial crisis or disaster. With each of these losses, we need to give ourselves some time and space to grieve, and surround ourselves with people who are supportive through the process. It is important that we go *through* our season of grieving, but not set up a tent and camp out in our grief for a lifetime. Once we go through the process, we will have a tremendous amount of compassion for anyone we meet who is going through similar things in the Wilderness. We will "get it," where others may not understand. It builds in us the true Christ-like compassion for others as they go through their grieving.

There is a paradox that happens in this grieving period. People may be praying for us, and then all of sudden we feel joy for no reason. However, instead of welcoming the joy, we may not want to *feel* joyful. We may feel that by being joyful, it somehow negates the severity of what we are going through. This is not true, but it can feel like that at times. The Wilderness experience can be harsh and severe, but feeling joy does not negate the heaviness of the situation. If someone has done us wrong, it does not get them "off the hook." By being nice to that person, it does not release them from the accountability they have with the Lord and the things they have done. Choosing to let go of the hurt and anger we feel is not condoning the wrong done to us. God wants to deal with the situation in a way that brings about justice for us, yet mercy for those who may have hurt us. Our vindication does not mean the other person has to be punished. Holding on to our anger and hurt only keeps it alive, so that it continues to live on, to do damage every time we meditate on it.

> Choosing to let go of the hurt and anger we feel is not condoning the wrong done to us.

One of God's names in the Bible is *Jehovah-Gmolah*, which means, God of Recompense. When we choose to forgive or have joy, God will still recompense everything that has been stolen, lost, or destroyed in the Wilderness. When God brings back those things that were stolen, they will be far better than anything we let go of—whether we gave them up willingly or not. Embrace the joy-filled moments that come and realize that God is still the God of Recompense and will restore to you all that is lost.

In our days of grieving, we may feel like we need to take action. However, we need time to mourn, and when the process is over, move out as God leads. It is wise not to make any major decisions during severe emotional trauma.

BITTERNESS

Beware of becoming bitter in the Wilderness. Bitterness is tied to hopelessness. When we lose every thread of hope, then bitterness begins to settle into our spirit. At the root of bitterness is a belief that somehow things will never change, or that God has done us wrong. It begins with disappointment and grief, and when we do not deal with our pain at this level it grows into bitterness. It comes out in what we say over ourselves, others, and our situation. In the Wilderness it is imperative we keep a watchful check on our tongue. It is very easy to speak words of condemnation over ourselves or our situation. It is easy to roll off our tongue statements such as; "It is *ALWAYS* going to be this way," or "It is *NEVER* going to happen in my lifetime." We are pronouncing negative declarations over our lives when we say these types of statements. Bitterness has a way of sneaking up on us and gaining a foothold in our heart in the Wilderness, and will hinder what God is working out in our life.

When the Israelites were wandering in the Wilderness they did not find any water. When they finally found water, the water was bitter. They called the water *Marah* which means bitter. Their complaining turned into bitterness and their response quickly *became* their outward condition when they found the water to be bitter. The water was a representation of what was in their heart towards God. Their attitude matched their situation. The Israelites *believed* in their heart and *confessed* with their *mouth* the bitterness of their soul. If they had just hung on long enough, their next stop was a place called Elim. Elim had twelve refreshing springs of water and seventy date palms. Their next stop had water and dates, not just manna, which they had been complaining about.[18]

HANNAH

Hannah turned to God in her bitterness. Hannah was unable to have children and the other wife, Peninnah, would taunt her day and night about her barrenness. "She was in bitterness of soul, and prayed to the Lord and wept in anguish."[19] Hannah wept with grief, and was unable to eat because of her deep bitterness. One day she poured out her heart in prayer at the temple with so much sobbing that Eli (the prophet) thought she was drunk. She said she was not drunk, "For I have been praying out of *great anguish* and *sorrow*."[20] She was grieved in spirit. Even though she said she was bitter, she was in the temple praying, so on some level she still believed God could help her, otherwise she would not have been in the temple praying at all. She was still pouring out her heart to the Lord. This is the wrestling that happens in the Wilderness between our emotions, and what we are choosing to accept as truth. The Wilderness tests what we truly believe, and if we are willing to stand on the promises God gave us—even in spite of overwhelming circumstances and tremendous pain.

NAOMI

In the story of Naomi and Ruth, Naomi suffered great loss.[21] She had left her homeland, her husband died, both her sons died, and on top of all that she was now poor. Naomi was grieving and became bitter in her own personal Wilderness. She told her friends to no longer call her Naomi, but *Marah* which means *bitter*. Her despair and grief over the loss of her husband and both of her sons was too much to bear. She was bitter from the experience, but not embittered and hardened. *Embittered* is when our words and actions line up in a state of bitterness for an extended period of time. She had not completely given up hope. She still believed that God was faithful to His people. Her actions said something different than her words. She said one thing, but still acted in faith by coming back to Bethlehem, her home town. In spite of everything, she was a part of God's people and believed on some level that she would be blessed. Never once did God get angry at her in this story, for she was grieved in spirit from her great loss. In the face of tremendous loss, she still believed. If we look at Naomi at the end of her life we will see:

- A daughter-in-law (Ruth) who stuck by her side though she had her own grief.

- She became the mother-in-law to the richest man in town.

- She had her land back.

- Her family name was redeemed (from an Old Testament perspective on redeeming the land).

- She was now in the lineage of King David which is the linage of Christ.

Naomi said she went out *full* but came back *empty*, but at the end of her story she was completely *full* even though it did not look like that in the middle of her Wilderness. Eventually she had more than she could even think, imagine, or envision for her life. Not in her wildest dreams would she have conceived the plans that God had for her. This is true for us as well. Not in our wildest imaginations can we see all the plans that God has for us. We need to grieve our losses in the Wilderness, but know that God is *good* all the time, and the end of our story is still to come. God is not done yet!

Naomi and Hannah were conflicted and their emotions were raging, but they still kept their trust in God and their actions proved it. They confessed with their mouth, but did not truly believe in their heart what they were saying. Hannah spoke out of her emotions just like Naomi, but they both did not give up believing that God is good and He was going to come through for them. The danger in the Wilderness is confessing *what we feel*, instead of confessing *what the Word of God says* to be true. One of my friends, Susy, was watching the news on television and they were talking about the reporters that were embedded in the field of war. Then she felt like the Lord said to her, "Emotions are like embedded reporters. They report how we are feeling, but are powerless to help us." Our emotions are a gauge of our feelings, but they should not get a voice or have a say in the matter.

> The danger in the Wilderness is confessing what we feel, instead of confessing what the Word of God says to be true.

The basic premise we can hold onto through any Wilderness experience is that God is *good*. God is good no matter what the circumstances may be telling us. Trust that He is good and that He not only has a plan for our lives, but He knows how to bring it to pass as well. God is good *ALL* the time.

Jacob in the Bible is an example of wrestling with God through tough circumstances. When Jacob was headed back home to a hostile brother who wanted to kill him, he wrestled with God until daybreak.[22] He wanted God to bless him and he was not willing to go forward until he was blessed. The Wilderness is about wrestling with the words God has given us over our life until they come to pass. Declare them everyday. Put them on the door posts like the Scripture says. Keep them ever before our eyes and meditate on them. This is one of the keys to making it out of the Wilderness. The Bible says, "The Word is near you, *in your mouth* and in your heart—that is the Word of faith."[23] *Confess* with your mouth and *believe* in your heart. Whoever believes in Him shall not be disappointed. He is abounding in riches for all who call upon Him.

GET UP!

I own a company where there were many business deals that should have come to fruition, but because of other's disobedience they did not. This was a faith test for me. Did I still trust God? Did I still believe God would provide for me and my family? Was I willing to forgive and not let it become an offense? In my business dealings there was *betrayal* followed by *grief*.

People presented themselves to be different than they really were. Mostly, I grieved the loss of integrity of other Christian business people and the deals that should have been. The "should-have-beens," and the "it's-not-fairs" pounded in my mind constantly, like a dripping faucet. What hurt the most was it came from people claiming to be Christians. As I was in this grieving stage, God told me, "Stop grieving over them. Pick up your oil and go anoint your David." God led me to the story of Samuel who had anointed Saul king over Israel. Samuel liked Saul and was close to him, but Saul was disobedient, so God was about to choose another king named David to take his place. "Now the Lord said to Samuel, '*How long will you grieve over Saul*, since I have rejected him from being king over Israel?' *Fill your horn with oil and go*, I will send you to Jesse the Bethlehemite, for I have selected a king for Myself among his sons."[24]

When God said to stop grieving and pick up my oil, He was telling me to stop grieving the loss of the business deals and continue to move forward. It did not matter if they were Christians or not, I needed to forgive them and keep moving forward, despite the setback or delay. "To pick up my oil" meant to forgive them, and continue moving forward trusting God for His provision in future deals. I was not to give up because some deals did not work out.

The grieving process has different steps that we must move through, but there is a time in the process where God says, "Get up. Stop grieving, and get moving into your destiny. I have divine appointments waiting for you, but you need to stop camping out in this grief and move forward." I am by no means minimizing the grieving process. There is a time to grieve, but then there is a time when we need to leave those places of grief and press forward towards our own personal Promised Land. Grieving is good and healthy, but we are not to spend a lifetime there when it was only meant for a season. There is "a time to cry and a time to laugh. A time to grieve and a time to dance."[25] Each has their place and their season.

> **Get up. Stop grieving, and get moving into your destiny.**

There are examples in the Bible when God gave this same message to His leaders. Moses had his face to the ground, not knowing what to do when Pharaoh's army had chased him to the Red Sea. With his back against the wall at the Red Sea, God basically said, "Why are you on your face? Get up—point

147

your staff, part the Red Sea, and cross over." God said, "Why are you crying out to Me? Tell the people to get moving!"[26] Joshua did the same thing in a city called Ai after the Israelites crossed the Jordan. When they lost that battle, Joshua had his face to the ground grieving the loss of the battle when God said, "Get up, for there is sin in the camp." He was to deal with the sin and then go back in battle to win the war.[27] We may lose a battle here and there, but get back up and keep going— God has already won the war!

When the season of grieving is over, we need to get up and move forward into the next phase God has for us. For some of us it will be a short time of grieving. For others it may be a lot longer, depending on what things we have gone through in our own personal Wilderness time. Some are bigger losses than others. Some of the losses may include the loss of a dream or a loss of an expectation. But God is shifting the way we view a "loss" by bringing us into a new place, and shifting old mindsets that have kept us bound. One time the Lord told me through a friend, "Your loss will not be *collateral damage*." What they meant by this was the loss of some things in the Wilderness may not be permanent, and some things which seem *gone* will be resurrected, or they may come back in a better way.

The Wilderness will shift our expectations and realign *our* dreams to *His* dreams for our lives. A key is to trust that God will lead us to a better place, even if it means letting go of things near and dear to our hearts. There *IS* an end to this season in our life. It may not seem like it at the time, but this too shall pass, and we will make it to the other side.

OUR PRAYER TO GOD

God,

I ask for forgiveness for those times when I have grumbled about being in the Wilderness, or for the times I have complained about things that have been lost. I ask You, Holy Spirit, to be my Comforter and renew my strength during this time. You said to come to You when we are weary and heavy-laden, and You will give us rest.

Thank You that You became a man and knew sorrows and were familiar with grief. You understand all that I am going through, and You are faithful to be there in my darkest hour. I choose to believe with my heart and confess with my mouth, that You are more than willing and able to help me through this time in the Wilderness. I will no longer complain to others, but only pour out my complaint to You with full expectation that You will hear me when I cry. For You are a loving Father and care for Your children. I will offer to You a sacrifice of praise everyday.

Amen

GOD'S PRAYER TO US

My Child,

You are My beloved and My banner over you is love. It has always been love, will always be love, and is love for eternity. I came down to earth and took on the form of a servant in the likeness of a man to feel what you are feeling, and to experience what you are experiencing. I, too, faced grief when My friend died. I, too, faced utter grief when the Father turned His face from me when I was on the cross. I know the grief you are experiencing, and I chose to lay down My life for you. But what I laid down, I chose to pick back up through resurrection power. I will resurrect expectations that have died in your Wilderness time. There will be NO collateral damage!

Trust Me to take you by the hand and lead you out of your Wilderness. It may not be the way you thought, but you are coming out, even if it seems like it will never end. There is an end to this season, but stay the course until I have finished the work I am accomplishing in you. Trust Me and speak aloud those things that I have spoken about you and your circumstances. Turn to Me and lean on Me, for My love covers you. My yoke is easy, and My burden is light. Speak and it shall be, believe and it shall come to pass. I will be a pillar of cloud by day, and a fire by night, to lead you out into an expansive place. Trust Me to lead you out. Daily speak those things that I have spoken over you. Stay in agreement with My Word and you will come forth in victory and with more power and authority than you can imagine.

Love,
Jehovah-Gmolah
God of Recompense

STUDY GUIDE

1. The best antidote to complaining is praise and worship. Put on some praise music and take some time each day to worship God. On YouTube.com you can create your own free play list of any Christian songs they offer. You can loop it and have it playing all day long on your computer or electronic device. They have a huge selection of songs. Pandora.com also allows you to create free radio stations and you can have stations with worship music from many genres.

2. Is there anything that you have been complaining about this week? Ask God to forgive you for complaining and give it to Him. Trust Him to correct the situation you are complaining about.

3. Are you grieving the loss of anything in the Wilderness? There may be several losses. It may be a material item, loss of a marriage, or it may be the loss of a dream or an expectation. Grieve the loss. Many people skip right over this step, but it is an extremely important process to go through. Some churches have grief recovery support groups to help you through losses in your life. It is worthwhile to search one out.

4. Forgive anyone that has done you wrong in the Wilderness, so that you do not give the enemy any type of foothold in your life. Remember, holding on to our anger and hurt only keeps it alive to do damage to us (not them) every time we meditate on it.

END NOTES

1. Midbar. *Strong's Exhaustive Concordance: New American Standard Bible.* Retrieved from http://www.blueletterbible.org.
2. Midbar. *Strong's Exhaustive Concordance: New American Standard Bible.* Retrieved from http://www.blueletterbible.org.
3. Matthew 12:34-37 (NASB, Emphasis added).
4. Psalm 142:2 (NIV).
5. Numbers 13:33b (NASB, Emphasis added).
6. Numbers 14:37 (NASB).
7. Matthew 8:2-3a (NIV, Emphasis added).
8. Grumbling. The Free Dictionary by Farlex. Retrieved from http://www.thefreedictionary.com/grumbling.
9. Murmur. *Merriam-Webster's Dictionary.* Retrieved from http://www.merriam-webster.com/dictionary/murmur.
10. Psalm 45:1b (KJV, Emphasis added).
11. Exodus 14:12b (NASB, Emphasis added).
12. Matthew 18:19-20.
13. Psalm 23:4 (NIV, Emphasis added).
14. Acts 2:26b (AMP, Emphasis added).
15. Psalm 30:5b (NIV Emphasis added).
16. Psalm 43:5 (AMP).
17. Isaiah 53:4.

18. Numbers 33:9.
19. I Samuel 1:10 (NKJV).
20. I Samuel 1:16b (NLT, Emphasis added).
21. See the book of Ruth for the whole story of Naomi.
22. See Genesis 32.
23. Romans 10:8 (NASB, Emphasis added).
24. 1 Samuel 16:1 (NASB, Emphasis added).
25. Ecclesiastes 3:4 (NLT).
26. Exodus 14:15b (NLT).
27. See Joshua 7:10.

CHAPTER SEVEN

DECLARATIONS

"O Lord, open my lips,
that my mouth may declare Your praise."
Psalm 51:15 (NASB)

Several years ago, I learned about making declarations over my life. A *declaration* is proclaiming something verbally over ourselves *aloud* that God has said about us either in His Word, or something that He spoke to our heart. There is power when His Word is said *aloud*. One of my friends, Carol, got a Word from the Lord that said, "My Word out of ***My*** mouth, is not diminished when it becomes My Word out of **your** mouth." His Word is powerful whether He says it or we say it. "My Word that goes out from my mouth, it will not return to me empty, but will accomplish what I desire and achieve the purpose for which I sent it."[1]

I decided to take some promises God had given me from His Word and had spoken to me personally, and wrote them down as declarations. I wrote each declaration on one page so they were easy to speak aloud. This is an excellent way to begin lining up your words with what God says about your situation. I would speak those declarations aloud over my life every morning. It was very empowering and encouraged me in my faith. There were times when I could really wrap myself around those words and believe them. Other times, it took everything I had just to be obedient to declare them, even though I struggled to believe them.

A few years later, I noticed a decidedly different tone in the way I said my declarations each morning. My voice and tone were different in the way I spoke them. I was beginning to believe what I was saying. Every year I would update my declarations and begin again with the new "bigger" word. Previously, the declarations served to build up my faith to believe the big things I was standing for, but there was a change that happened. I began to declare them because I *did* believe them. Somewhere in those two years a shift occurred. God had worked on the inside of me so that I no longer said the words *to* believe—I said the words *because* I believed! The more I spoke the declarations aloud, the more they sank deeper and deeper into my spirit until I really believed what I was declaring.

156

Declarations are things that have been untested in us and are waiting to be manifested. We have not done those big things yet, so how do we know that we can do them? It is through the grace of God and not the law that we can do those great exploits for Him. In saying our declarations every day, they become a great deterrent from complaining about our circumstances. When we begin to thank God and declare the good things that He has in store for us, we begin to believe them and complaining falls by the wayside. *For where our words travel our hearts will soon follow.*

> **Declarations are things that have been untested in us and are waiting to be manifested.**

Declarations also bring our mind back from wandering. Ilene Gregorian, a teacher in an attention training class said, "Mindfulness techniques vary, but the intent is the same—controlling attention and clearing the mind of distractions. You can take yourself down with your thoughts faster than any enemy can. Your thoughts are secondary. That is just chatter. Your attention and awareness are primary."[2] Declarations can help us put a "spam filter" in our heads. We need to set our direction toward the future and what God has for us, and declare it to the heavens every day and watch Him open the flood gates.

WHO SPEAKS INTO OUR LIFE

Who are we allowing to speak into our lives? Who are we partnering with in business or friendships? It is important for us to be a part of a group of believers who believe *for* and *with* us. This is a core group of believers who believe we can overcome our circumstances and come out of the Wilderness, not those who talk the doom and gloom of the world's economies. Fellow believers who have the same mindset are invaluable and can encourage us in the hardest of times.

DESPITE THE CIRCUMSTANCES

The old saying about courage is "do it afraid." The word for the Wilderness is "do it despite of" (despite of the circumstances). Worship despite how we feel. Pray despite what is going on. Make a vocal and conscious decision to "choose to believe" despite what is happening all around.

There were many days in my Wilderness journey when I said to the Lord, "I do not know about tomorrow, and yesterday is gone. But despite the circumstances, I choose to believe for today. I cannot promise You tomorrow, but today I choose to believe." I would do this many times a day just to get my mind and spirit in alignment. The Wilderness can be so daunting—it is hard to think past today. We need to give God our today and choose to believe despite it all.

One day I was praying and thanking God for the good things that were coming once I was out of the Wilderness. I prayed for the good things that He had planned for my family, and the good things that were in my future. He abruptly stopped me in the middle of this seemly "good" prayer and said, "Be careful what you call good." I was thanking Him for future things that were going to happen that were good, but what He was trying to get across to me is that life is good now. No matter where we are or the circumstances that we find ourselves in, it is good. He has the heart of a loving father. He cares for us and He is good all the time! "This is the day that the Lord has made; let us rejoice and be glad in it."[3] So the good is for us right now (here) in the Wilderness, not only when we are out and moving on to the next leg of the journey.

Being an "A" type personality, I used to get very upset at people who said to "enjoy the journey." But the deeper I traveled in my own Wilderness, the more I realized the value of the process in the journey. I began to understand how much of a good work God is doing now. Hope means a joyful expectation of good. We can have hope because we can trust God to do what He has promised. He is the Good Shepherd and He laid down His life for the sheep. He is good all the time. We need to learn to speak into those circumstances which are contrary to God's truth. When we see the Wilderness for what it truly is, we can treat the Wilderness time with respect.

He gave us an example of this when He spoke to the wind and the waves on the sea. We can speak to our circumstances as well.

THE RICE EXPERIMENT

My children and I did an experiment to prove the power of God's Word. We based our experiment on the Scripture that says, "Death and life are in the power of the tongue."[4] We took identical glass containers and put the same amount of cooked rice into each jar. On one jar we wrote the words "You are cursed and you will mold quickly." On the other jar we wrote, "You are blessed and will last a long time." We placed both jars in the same part of the house to be equal in the amount of light and heat they would receive. Every day when each of us saw the rice we would either bless or curse the rice aloud, depending on what it said on the container. Within a week, the cursed rice was molding and rotting. The blessed rice was still white and clean with no mold.

I told my friend about this test, so she tried it as well. She did the same experiment. However, she put the same amount of rice into only one container and split the rice inside, pushing half the rice to one side and the remainder to the other side. She cursed one side and blessed the other. Within a few days the cursed rice was moldy and the blessed rice was fine. They were both in the same container! It was amazing! My children's faith grew exponentially because of this exercise. We had said we believed the Scripture about our tongue. Now we REALLY believed this Scripture! We actually physically proved it.

Then my friend did another experiment where she stood on the Scripture, "If two of you agree here on earth concerning anything you ask, my Father in heaven will do it for you."[5] My friend prayed in agreement with her granddaughter that within three days the rice would mold. On exactly the third day the rice became moldy. The rice responded to her prayers immediately. So too, in our own lives when we pray, the Lord hears our prayers immediately.

For *rice* there is no "interference" to hinder the prayers, because it is just rice with no will of its own. In our prayers for people or situations, answers sometimes take longer. The *upward leg* of our prayers goes straight to the throne room of God. But it is on the *downward leg* of God's answers that the enemy fights us. Daniel prayed and his prayers were heard immediately (upward leg), but there was a twenty-one day delay because the angels were warring in heaven (downward leg).[6] It is in the journey coming back down when heaven meets hell in the atmosphere and the resistance begins.

WORDS MATTER

We can pray to God and begin asking Him through the Holy Spirit to reveal and convict us of the words that are coming from our own mouth which are not of Him. Many times we do not even realize we are speaking words contrary to what God has told us. Having a friend who will tell us when we are saying contrary things is invaluable. I have trained my own family members to remind me when I start complaining or grumbling. They *"call me out"* on this quite a bit. Friends can help as well with blind spots we have. Part of the experience in the Wilderness is getting our heads and hearts to line up with our mouths. What we bless, God blesses. What we curse, God curses. What we bind is bound, and what we loose is now open.

> We can pray to God and begin asking Him through the Holy Spirit to reveal and convict us of the words that are coming from our own mouth which are not of Him.

God calls those things that are not as though they are. He *spoke* over Gideon and said, "O' Mighty man of valor!"[7] The word valor in the Hebrew means; strength, might, efficiency, wealth, and army. In the Webster's dictionary it means heroic and full of courage. Gideon was hiding in the wine press when God said "O' Mighty man of valor." God *spoke* the word *valor* over his life though Gideon was acting in a manner contrary to that word by hiding in the wine press. God calls those characteristics that are buried deep inside of us into the light for us to consider, ponder, and to begin to speak over ourselves. What has God spoken over your life that you need to begin to pay attention to? Declare those things every day until you become fully convinced they are true.

SAMPLE DECLARATIONS

There are examples in the Bible of declarations we can speak over our own lives. Here are some Scriptures I have turned into declarations to illustrate how you can create your own. One resource I recommend is *www.BlueLetterBible.org*. You can look up any word in the original language and get its definition. That is what I did for the Scriptures below.

JOEL 2:25 - DECLARATION

"Thank you God that you will make up to me for the years that I have been beset and surrounded, and for things in my

163

life-changing because of prolonged stress, deprived of what rightfully belongs to me. I trust You will replace those areas that have been torn down, and worn away. No longer will anyone plague me or be a source of vexation."

MALACHI 3:11 - DECLARATION

"Thank you Lord that you rebuke the devourer that he may not destroy the dreams and visions that have been birthed in me— that I would not miscarry or abort my prosperity before it's time."

JOSHUA 1:8-9 - DECLARATION

I will not let what the Word of God says to me depart from my mouth. I will meditate on it at all times and do it! I will be prosperous, advance, succeed, be profitable, and have courage. I will be successful, shrewd in the management of practical affairs, having foresight in business, and will gain wealth. I will be strong and courageous, and will not be discouraged despite the circumstances, for the Lord my God is with me wherever I go.

Here are a few more samples of Scriptures in a longer format to help you get started creating your own declarations. Declare things over your life according to the Scriptures. It is important to quote Scriptures in your declarations because the Word is very powerful, alive, and active. It is as powerful as a double-edged sword so use it as your *offensive* weapon against the enemy every day.[8]

You may use these sample declarations to get started. Begin to ask God for specific promises He is giving you, and start to incorporate them into the samples below. You can create entirely different declarations that are specifically tailored for you.

HEALING DECLARATION
WRITTEN BY ORANGE COUNTY HEALING ROOM

Heavenly Father, I thank You for Your Living Word. You said that Your Word is life to those who find it, and medicine to all their flesh. Today, by my confession, I apply Your Word to my body by giving voice to it. You said in Psalm 139:14 that I am fearfully and wonderfully made, and Your works are marvelous. I declare that I was created by You, and I am a marvelous creation.

I speak to sickness and disease today and proclaim according to Philippians 2:10, that they must bow down to the mighty name of the Lord Jesus Christ. Every name in heaven, on earth, and under the earth bows its knee to Jesus' name.

I speak to my body today and declare that I have authority over it. I command it to receive the Word of God. Matthew 8:17 proclaims that Jesus bore my sicknesses and took my infirmities.

Heavenly Father, I thank You that the same Spirit that raised Jesus from the dead dwells in me and make me alive in my mortal body. I speak to my immune system (and anything else) and command it to line up with the Word of God. My immune system will destroy sickness and disease in my body and perform its job; for this is what God created it to do.

I thank You Father that every cell in my body responds to Your Word. Your Word permeates my body from the top of my head to the bottom of my feet. I confess that the Word of God is being made flesh in me. Psalm 103:3 declares that You, Father, forgave all my iniquities and healed all my diseases. Father, that is Your confession and I make it my confession also. I do not judge by the sight of my eyes, I judge by Your Living Word. It is Your Word that lives in me and brings health and healing to every part of my body.

Heavenly Father, I rejoice at your promise of divine health. You said it and I believe it! Today, I declare that I will see your promise of healing manifest in my body.

Healing is mine because Jesus paid the price two thousand years ago. God so loved the world that He sent His Son to die on the cross so that I could experience life on God's terms. His abundant life is manifesting in me, making me whole—body, soul, and spirit.

Amen.

HEALING DECLARATION
WRITTEN BY MELODIE FOX

Father, thank You for Your Word. It has the power and authority to transform and change, to heal and comfort, to deliver and set free. Whom the Son has set free, is free indeed! So I thank You that I am set free from any and all sickness and disease that tries to hinder me! I walk in freedom for that is why You have set me free! I stand in all the armor of God. Your Word is a sword that pierces through my doubt and unbelief. It is more powerful than a doubled-edged sword. Your Word does NOT go out void, but it accomplishes what it is sent out to do. I send Your Word out now and speak to my body. Rise up in health and strength! For I am fearfully and wonderfully made! I am humble, and I fear the Lord and shun evil.

This brings health to my body and nourishment to my bones. I received Your healing. By faith I am made whole. Father, I thank You for what Jesus did on the cross. He took all of my diseases and weaknesses upon Himself and by His wounds I am healed. You heal ALL of my diseases and crown me with love and compassion. Lord, there is NOTHING too difficult for You.

All my needs are met in You. My need of health and strength are met in You. Every one of your promises are "yes" and "amen" in Christ. I come against the spirit of doubt and unbelief in my life in Jesus' name. I bind anxiety and fear. You said perfect love casts out fear—and there is no fear in love.

Thank You that You loved me SO much you sent Jesus. I praise You, for You do ALL THINGS WELL-- I AM a new creature in Christ. Old things have passed away...ALL THINGS HAVE BECOME NEW. I walk in Your newness today.

OUR PRAYER TO GOD

God,

*Thank You that "**Your words** out of **Your mouth** are not diminished when **Your words** come out of **my mouth**." Forgive me for those times when I have complained and spoken contrary things over my life. I want to line up with Your Word and speak over my life those things You say about me, for "Your banner over me is love." I will begin to declare and decree Your promises every day as I soak in Your Word, because Your Word does not go out void. It produces all that it was sent to do. I commit my mouth to line up with what You say about me in all things and in all ways. I am truly and wonderfully made in your image, and I am healed by the stripes on Jesus' back. I am a new creation in Christ and all things have passed away. Behold, You are doing a new work in me. Thank You for Your love and for giving me Your Word. May I never take it for granted.*

Amen

GOD'S PRAYER TO US

My Child,

I love you with an unconditional love and sent My Word to you in flesh—Jesus. My Word goes forth as a lamp to your feet and a light for your path. You do not live by bread alone (or material things alone) but you live on everything that proceeds out of the mouth of God.

My Word goes out and will not return to Me empty without accomplishing what I desire, and will succeed in the matter for which I sent it. It will achieve the purpose I have for it. It is **MY** *job to watch over My Word to produce life and* **your** *job to speak it. All you need to do is appropriate My Word and put it in your mouth and watch your enemy scatter. Do this with all diligence and you will become a strong and powerful offensive weapon in My hand. Trust Me in this and do it often. Do it daily and watch how I turn around any contrary situation you face.*

Love,
El Shaddai
Lord God Almighty

STUDY GUIDE

1. Write a *Declaration* over your life. There are samples in this chapter to help you get started. Some thoughts on how to write a declaration:

   ● Pray and ask God to remind you of any verses in the Bible which have stood out in your devotional time with Him.

   ● Write those Scriptures down, personalize them, and string them together in the form of a Declaration.

   ● As you continue spending time in His Word, He will give you desires that come into your heart. He is the One who placed them there. Incorporate those desires into your Declaration as well.

   ● Write or type up your Declaration.

   ● Speak it aloud everyday.

   ● Commit it to memory.

As you begin to do this you will see a shift from simply saying the declaration *to* believe it, to saying it *because* you believe it! Update your Declarations periodically to make sure they are fresh and in alignment with what God is doing at each given time in your life.

2. The Holy Spirit is your best accountability partner. Ask Him to reveal those times when you are not speaking things which line up with the Word of God.

3. Pick a trusted friend who will let you know when you are complaining. This will help you be accountable for the words which come out of your mouth. Preferably choose someone with whom you spend a lot of time.

END NOTES

1. Isaiah 55:11b (NIV).
2. http://www.psmag.com/health/a-state-military-mind-42839/.
3. Psalm 118:24 (NIV).
4. Proverbs 18:21a (NASB).
5. Matthew 18:19b. (NLT).
6. See Daniel 10:13.
7. See Judges 6:12.
8. Hebrews 4:12.

CHAPTER EIGHT

CHARACTER BUILDING

*"Until the time came to fulfill his dreams,
the Lord tested Joseph's character."*
Psalm 105:19 (NLT)

The Wilderness can feel like Boot Camp. It is about doing things over and over and wondering why we are going around this mountain one more time. At times it feels like God is telling us to drop to the ground and give Him fifty more push-ups. But all the training is for a reason. It is to train us how to fight in war. It is training for a purpose, so that when we get to our Promised Land we will be able to take down the giants with a single blow, like David did with Goliath. David was in training when he was a boy watching his father's sheep. He took down a lion and a bear, and when it was time for Goliath, he came at him with the tenacity and courage of a young man well beyond his years.

This Wilderness Boot Camp is a season for building the necessary character in us to handle the next assignment God wants to release to us. Character is being built now in the Wilderness so we will be able to take down the enemy along the way, and conquer even bigger giants in our Promised Land. Some character traits that are being built in the Wilderness include: tenacity, trust, patience with endurance, and courage.

TENACITY

Tenacity is an important character trait that gets strengthened in the Wilderness. Tenacity is born in the womb of adversity. The definition of tenacity is *dogged persistence*, or *dour determination*. My friend once said in her Wilderness experience, "*It was either give up or rise up.* A tenacious spirit develops in the midst of the Wilderness. We must be tenacious to rise up into what we have been called to do, and submit to the stages we need to go through in order to get to our Promised Land. There comes a point in the process where we either believe God is who He says He is, or He is not. There is not much grey in the Wilderness.

The Scripture says, "Then all the congregation of the sons of Israel journeyed by stages from the Wilderness."[1] God told Moses to record each of the cities the Israelites traveled through in the forty years in the Wilderness. Each stage is important. We learn something from each place we are at in the Wilderness. We need to journal each stage of our travels in the Wilderness, and the things we have learned along the way. Looking back at what God has brought us through brings encouragement and builds our faith. Paying attention to what we have been through allows us to share it, in order to help others through their Wilderness experience. It is similar to the growth stages of a baby. When a baby is little, the first thing they learn to do is roll over on their stomach. Later they learn to crawl, and then walk. In some places where there are poisonous animals on the ground, many of the babies have skipped the crawling stage. Educators have now linked crawling with a part in the brain that helps children read. Those children that did not crawl had a hard time learning to read, and in some cases the children had to *go back* and learn to crawl (even though they were much older) just to help them read.

So too, in the Wilderness we need to go through each stage in the journey. If we skip this character building stage of developing a tenacious spirit, then there is a part of ourselves that is not fully developed to enter into the next assignment God has for us. The Children of Israel needed a tenacious spirit as they came out of the Wilderness, so that when they went into their Promised Land they would not give up. The Scripture says, "I (God) will not drive them out (the enemy) before you in a single year, that the land may not become desolate and the beast of the field become too numerous for you. I will drive them out before you little by little until you become fruitful and take possession of the land."[2] In today's vernacular, we do not get physically attacked by beasts of the field, but it is a metaphor for those things that can come against and take us down as we go into our Promised Land.

My son is a good example of this. He is very gifted and has a high degree of intelligence. Getting "A's" in school comes very easy to him. I have noticed that when he does not understand a new concept within a couple minutes (which is normal for him), he gets frustrated and does not want to complete the task. He tends to give up. His character development of a tenacious spirit has not yet caught up to his high degree of intelligence. Because he has "conquered the land of school work" so quickly, he is consumed and overwhelmed at times when something new (like encountering the beast of the field) is not conquered so fast.

Many times when people have things come easily to them or have been promoted quickly in some area, they end up "crashing and burning" because their character cannot withstand the pressure at the top. There are many stories about someone who has won millions of dollars in the lottery, only to end up losing all the money within a few short years. They did not have the character development or financial skills to manage what was suddenly entrusted to them.

It is similar to climbers that hike Mt. Everest. They need to get to Base Camp #1 and stay there for four weeks before they go to Base Camp #2, and so on. Their body has to acclimate in stages to the lack of oxygen they will experience at the top of the mountain. So too, when God is pulling us into our destiny to the top of our mountain, we need to take it in steps and degrees. Most overnight successes were years in the making!

Most overnight successes were years in the making!

We need to develop this tenacious spirit or we will have a missing piece going into the next part of our journey. This will mean taking another lap around the desert. The goal is to go through every stage *even if it is painful or unpleasant*, because we do not want to come back and go through this Boot Camp one more time. Be patient and wait for God, because He does not want to release us too soon and have us come back to this place of training again.

It is not always easy going through each stage, but each step is critical to completing the process that He has begun in us. Each step is necessary so that we do not stunt our own growth in the things God has for us.

NO OVERNIGHT SUCCESS

For every mountain top experience, there is a deep and abiding process that proceeded that moment. There are no overnight successes, only years of working out our faith to have it surface in an instant. It is the "suddenlys" in the Bible. It is when God shows up *suddenly* to perform a miracle, even though the person has been standing for their healing for years. If our character is not built up to the point of handling the *suddenly,* then we will crash and burn, or at the very least disqualify ourselves in the games for awhile. *Suddenly* Abraham had a son named Isaac, but it was *twenty-five years* in the making. *Suddenly* Joseph was out of jail facing Pharaoh, but it was after *thirteen years* spent as an Egyptian slave. *Suddenlys* come quickly, but they are years in the making.

At times in the Wilderness it takes sheer tenacity and guts to keep going no matter what. It is a conscientious *choice* of the mind, heart, and spirit to believe. It is a *choice* to believe despite the circumstances, despite the report of the doctors, despite the current economic condition. Above all else, *TODAY I choose* to believe.

CARRY OUR OWN OIL

This season in the Wilderness is about carrying our own oil. In the past we may have looked to others for all of our prayer support—neglecting to pray for ourselves as much as we should have.

There is a story in the Bible about ten brides who took their lamps and oil and waited for the bridegroom.[3] Half the women had enough oil for the entire night until the bridegroom came, and the other half ran out of oil. The ones that did not have enough oil had to leave to go buy oil, and they missed the bridegroom's return. The Body of Christ is going through a season where we need to each carry our own oil. It is easy to go in search of the latest teacher, prayer warrior, tape series, or someone to give us a Word from the Lord. But *NOW* is the time when each of us needs to carry our *OWN* oil. We cannot share it with others because they need to carry it themselves. Now is the time to press in like never before. In the Wilderness we cannot rely on someone else's faith to pull us up or get us through. Sure we all have friends that give us support, but our ultimate source comes from God alone. Our faith grows deeper in the Lord as we press in to Him during this time.

Some people do not carry their own oil, and want to throw a *pity party.* They want us to feel sorry for them and they talk about how their situation is so much worse than ours. They pull on us too much. As long as this attitude is prevalent, the Promised Land is in the distant future for them. Carrying our own oil means pressing in and spending time with God in His Word. We must spend time in prayer, in the secret place, with the Lord alone. We need to come with an *expectation* that we will hear from Him. Quietly waiting for His response and learning to partner with Him in what He is about to do is an art that is refined in the Wilderness experience.

It is tempting to "rescue" someone who is in the Wilderness. We see their pain and want to help. But if we do, it will not build the tenacity they need for their next phase of development. It is like rescuing a caterpillar out of its cocoon before it's time. The caterpillar builds its strength in its wings to fly by fighting to get out of the cocoon. So too, when we are in the Wilderness we are strengthening our wings for the next phase. It takes resistance to make us stronger and the tenacity to keep going despite the odds, which develops the necessary level of character to enter into the Promised Land.

EMBRACE THE WILDERNESS

A friend called me one day and told me to "Embrace the Wilderness." I thought they were absolutely *crazy* for even suggesting such a thing. My thoughts had always been, "When is this ever going to end?" They encouraged me to pray to God during the Wilderness experience this simple yet difficult prayer: "God, I will be here in this Wilderness as long as it takes to build the character in me for where You are taking me." It is a gutsy prayer—one that takes total surrender and complete trust.

> "God, I will be here in this Wilderness as long as it takes to build the character in me for where You are taking me."

Submitting our will to the Lord and asking Him to keep us in the Wilderness for *as long it takes*, is a huge paradigm shift in our thinking. It takes complete trust that God will take care of us even through the pain. The focus becomes, "Do Your work in me God because You are in control *AND* I *trust* You completely." God wants to develop our character so that we can sustain the level of success that is coming to us in the form of our destiny.

It is one thing to gain a victory, but quite another to occupy territory once you get it. The difference between the two is the strength of the character of the person. I have heard it said many times, "In life our biggest temptations do not come when we are in poverty, but when we have wealth." Wealth, success, and power have an allure that is captivating, if it is not subdued under God's authority over us. It is in the high places that it is the hardest to stay pure, not in the valleys. God is building in us the capacity to fully trust Him no matter what the consequences, and to expand ourselves even if it is painful at times.

It is similar to a woman in labor. When a woman gives birth, she needs to dilate and expand in order to make room for the new child that is coming. This needs to happen first, before she "pushes" or "presses in." It sounds counterintuitive, but actually *embracing the pain* of the process helps us to expand and dilate. That is why midwives are a huge asset in the birthing process. They help the woman relax and expand to get ready for the birth that is about to come. In childbirth most women do not dilate from zero to five centimeters within minutes. Usually it requires hours of dilating and working with the contractions to push the baby down the birthing canal to its final destination. This is true for us in the Wilderness. We do not race through the Wilderness in a matter of days, but it is months, and sometimes years in the making. The Wilderness is about being expanded in order to birth the next level of our journey.

The Scripture says, "Enlarge the place of your tent, stretch your tent curtains wide, do not hold back; lengthen your cords, strengthen your stakes."[4] We are being stretched beyond what is comfortable and being pulled in a new direction that we have never been before. But we are stretched for a divine purpose, not just for the sake of being in pain, but pain for a *purpose*. It is in our deepest pain that flows out of us our deepest passion.

God is developing the *character* within the character. We are the main character in the the story of our lives. The depth of our character is birthed through the pain in the Wilderness. The Bible says, "My righteous one shall live by faith; and if He shrinks back, my soul has no pleasure in Him. But we are not of those who shrink back to destruction, but of those who have faith to the preserving of the soul."[5] Jesus is our example. He submitted Himself to the Father and completely trusted Him even to the point of death. When Jesus was at the Garden of Gethsemane He said, "Father, if You are willing, remove this cup from Me; yet not My will, but Yours be done."[6] He was in great agony, but then it says, "Now an angel from heaven appeared to Him, strengthening Him."[7] Jesus was basically saying, "I do not want to go through this, and yes I do want it to end right now, but not My will but Yours be done so that You can accomplish all that You want to do through Me."

Ministering angels came to Him when He was in the Garden of Gethsemane, and also when He was in the Wilderness for forty days when the devil tempted Him. In the Wilderness we are not alone. God will send His ministering angels to help us through the process and the journey that we are embarking on. Even when we go through painful things in the Wilderness, God comforts us and sends us people, angels, or signs to strengthen us for the journey that is ahead. It may not be a "quick work," but He will give His angles charge over us and minister to us along the way. They will calm our fears and give us peace as we progress through the Wilderness.

The challenge is getting to the point in our journey when we can say, "God I am here in this Wilderness. I will be here until you have completed the work in me that needs to happen before I come out. Change me Lord and do your work so that I will have the character to occupy the territory that we have conquered. I want to be free to enter into the next leg of my journey without hindrance from within." That is a very hard statement to make, but one that will completely shift our focus and build trust. It is a statement to fully surrender to God and completely gives up

> I want to be free to enter into the next leg of my journey without hindrance from within.

any sort of control. Once that happens we will find a new-found freedom, because we will be under His covering.

TRUST VERSES A SPIRIT OF CONTROL

A simple statement, yet hard to believe at times, is that God is *trustworthy.* Said another way, He is *worthy of our trust.* It is not knowing in our mind, but "knowing" in our spirit. We can trust Him. One way to tell if we truly trust Him is to measure how much *control* we need in a given situation. Giving up a *spirit of control* is a byproduct of believing in God and *trusting* Him that He has our best interest at heart.

Making it through the Wilderness means giving up control and trusting Him to take care of us completely. I heard it said, "We are not wired to have control, but we are wired to have responsibilities." Control issues arise many times when there has been trauma in our childhood. If there was abuse or neglect, or we felt manipulated, then a spirit of control can surface which breeds a spirit of self-reliance. Self-reliance can cross the line into rebellion when we are not trusting God fully. It may also be hard to trust people. The people who were supposed to care about us the most did not, so whom can we trust? These issues then (either consciously or unconsciously) get placed on God. When we take back control, in essence we are saying, "I need to control the situations that arise, and I cannot trust God to be there for me." This is completely false! God is worthy of ALL of our trust. The essence of who He is exudes His love and He is a good God. It is a foundational level truth that needs to sink down deep into our spirit.

Control means trying to have power over the circumstances, but it can also mean controlling the *timing* of getting out. I struggled with this during my Wilderness experience. I kept thinking if I was totally on my best behavior and 100% obedient to God, this would somehow speed up my journey through the Wilderness. I wanted to *control the timing* in the Wilderness. Only God controls the timing. Yes, obedience is important and disobedience can slow down the process, but that fact is this: *it is a process* that we must go through. Process events are key to forming us in the Wilderness. God told the Israelites when they were supposed to go forward with Him, and whenever they chose to go on without Him, it was disastrous.

The spiritual root of all control issues is a *lack of trust*. "Do you trust Me?" says the Lord. "If I tell you to move to the right or to the left—to stop or to go—will you do it and *trust* Me? Will you do it, even if you do not understand? Will you do it, even if it makes you look ridiculous?" We need to trust God no matter what, and leave the results up to Him."

ENDURANCE WITH PATIENCE

"Endurance develops strength of character in us."[8] "For you have need of *endurance*, so that when you have done the will of God, you may receive what was promised."[9] We need endurance to continue on and come out of the Wilderness.

At times we need to wait and rest in the fact that God is not late. "For the vision is yet for the appointed time; It hastens toward the goal and it will not fail. Though it tarries, wait for it; For it will certainly come, it will not delay."[10] Keeping a right attitude through the Wilderness is critical. It is our attitude and obedience through the Wilderness that will affect how we come out—either through the Promised Land, or six feet under our circumstances. We need to rise above our circumstances and allow the Lord to do His full work in our life.

Some stages are short, while others are long. In the Wilderness the Children of Israel followed the pillar of cloud by day and the fire by night. They only moved through the desert when God moved. Sometimes they packed up their camp and

> **It is our attitude and obedience through the Wilderness that will affect how we come out—either through the Promised Land, or six feet under our circumstances.**

187

moved quickly, while at other times the Scriptures say they stayed for years in one spot.

Endurance is like a surfer on the water who paddles out to catch a wave. He gets hit from the incoming waves of his circumstances, but his goal is to paddle to "the outside break." He endures with *patience* the oncoming waves that hit him in cycles. He continues to paddle out despite getting hit from the waves. He dips his head under the waves to finally get to the outside break. He waits and lines up for the right wave of opportunity. He has *patience* and waits as long as it takes to find the perfect wave. As the right wave begins to peak, he paddles to get into the momentum as the wave breaks, and then rides it to shore.

This is what God is having us do in the Wilderness. The work is in paddling out to the wave. We have to push through every hindrance that comes against us to get out to the "line up" and rest. We push through so that we can rest.

We continue to move forward despite being hit at every turn, and we patiently keep moving forward despite getting hit by the waves of adverse circumstances. But once we hit the top, we will be able to ride in the wave at just the right time into our Promised Land.

Just like the surfer who waits and scans the horizon to look for that perfect wave and gets into position, so too when we are resting in God. He will realign us and get us into position to catch His plans and purpose for us during this time. The power of the wave is the authority and velocity that He is giving us, and it will carry us to shore. We will be at the right place at the right time to accomplish all that He wants us to do.

Jim Caviezel, the actor who played Jesus in *The Passion* said, "If you do not pick up your cross and follow Him, then you will be crushed under the weight of it." One way of picking up our cross is patiently submitting to the work that God wants to do in us in the Wilderness. Not in the crying, "Uncle ... Uncle" sort of way where we will do anything to "get out," but rather a full surrender to "stay in" through the entire process and let Him accomplish the work He is doing. We must develop and mature so that we are not tripped up in the next leg of our journey. It is not a quick work. It is not a microwave experience where God just zaps us and "Bam!" we are ready to come out like piping hot bread. It is a day-to-day reliance on the *Bread of Life*. It is the patience to get our manna daily (and only enough for that day), as we work through the process of being in the desert.

During this endurance phase of the Wilderness, I have said some things to the Lord out of desperation.

One time I told God, "Just throw me a *bone* would you?"

In which He replied, "I am giving you a *steak!*"

It is all about perspective. The character He brings in our lives is the *steak*, but many times all we want to settle for is a *bone—right now!* He is *giving to us* far more than we are *giving up* in the Wilderness. We can be focusing on the here and now, but He is focusing on manifesting our future and building the character in us to sustain the growth that is about to happen. This character building time is necessary for the birth of the new move He is doing in our lives.

COURAGE

"Courage does not always roar. Sometimes it is the quiet voice at the end of the day that says: 'I will try again tomorrow.'"[11] In the Wilderness, courage is getting up each day and deciding to do life one more time. We need hope in order to have the courage to keep going. The Scripture says, "Having hope will give you courage. You will be protected and will rest in safety."[12]

We have tremendous weapons that God has given us in our arsenal. "For the weapons of our warfare are not carnal, but mighty in God for pulling down strongholds."[13] We do not shrink back. We press in *despite* the circumstances. We need to press in until we finally arrive in our Promised Land. From God's perspective it is not in the "arriving," but is in the act of "pressing in." For when we press in we are like an eagle in front of a fan that builds up strength in its wings. It is the "pressing in," not necessarily, in the "winning" of the battle. It is in the "pressing in" and standing that we get stronger. Stand in courage for what is right no matter the odds—no matter what the crowd says—no matter what others around us say. It is in the standing and pressing in that the victory is found, and it is a victory like no other. It is a victory of the heart. It is a deepening of character. It is not necessarily a worldly victory. That is why movies like *Gladiator* and *Braveheart* penetrate to the soul. The main character in the movie presses in *despite* terrible circumstances, *despite* the roar of the crowd. They *run to the roar* and face the odds no matter what those closest to them may say. It matters only what God says.

RUN TO THE ROAR

In the jungle, a male lion will stand at one end of a field and roar. The natural tendency of prey is to run away from the roar, but when they do they are running straight into a trap. There are a group of female lions ready at the other end of the field waiting for the prey to run into their ambush. "Running to the roar" means we have the courage to run straight towards our fear. We give it no place and no power in our lives. One example would be to tithe even though we are having a hard time paying the bills. We hit our fear head on and continue to prove God in the tithe. The Scripture talks about testing God in the tithe. It says, "'Bring the whole tithe into the storehouse, so that there may be food in My house, and *test* Me now in this,' says the Lord of host, 'if I will not open for you the windows of heaven, and pour out for you the blessing until it overflows.'"[14]

It seems counterintuitive, but that is exactly what Elijah did with the widow in the Bible. God sent him to a widow to provide for him. He went to her probably thinking she was a rich widow, but he ended up with a widow that was making her last meal with her son and planned to die. He asked for her last meal and when she gave it to him, the oil and flour reproduced miraculously and all of them lived off that oil and flour during the entire time of the drought.

Another way to "run to roar" is to believe in healing, despite the bad report we may have received. Instead of praying, "If it be Thy will" prayers, stand on the Scripture that says, "He was pierced for our rebellion, crushed for our sins. He was beaten so we could be whole. He was whipped so we could be *healed*."[15] Instead of getting fearful of a doctor's report, continue to speak Scriptures over the situation. It is God's will to heal every time!

The Scriptures back up this statement. Run to the roar and stand for health.

FEAR is the *enemy's* roar. *COURAGE* is *our* roar. We need to roar even louder. Our roar silences the enemy and gives him paralysis so he cannot move into our territory, or come against those in our pride. Roar with the verbosity and ferocity that will strike at the heart of the enemy. Run to the Roar!

PRESSING IN TO OVERCOME FEAR

Courage is overcoming our fear. One of the ways to overcome fear is by getting more *offensive* in our tactics with the enemy. For years I was on the defense and fear reined in my life. Fear was a *"trusted friend"* and I played a defensive game in life. It is similar to only waiting for Jesus' return, but not offensively taking territory for His kingdom. God gave me the picture of a football game. The coaches on the opposing team watch the tapes of the game to see how the opponents play. Some teams are more defensive in nature, while others are more offensive. The enemy is sitting in the coach's room watching our tapes and he knows our every move. We can become predictable because many of us play a defensive game. A defensive game is played by saying prayers that usually start with the words, "Oh God." For example, "Oh God, please help me get out of this mess that I am in." Or, "Oh God, please help my family member," or, "If you will only do this one thing for me, I will serve you the rest of my life."

Now is the season to begin taking territory and getting offensive in our prayers. We have the power in Jesus' name to bind and to loose. The Scripture says, "I will give you the keys of the kingdom of heaven; and whatever you bind on earth will be bound in heaven, whatever you loose on earth will be loosed in heaven."[16] There is an important sequential order in this Scripture. It is important to bind things first and then loose. Getting on the offensive is saying things such as; "I bind the enemy from any kind of sickness that has come upon my child, and I loose health, healing, and wholeness in those parts of his body that need healing." This would be a more offensive manner of prayer. This is much more effective than the "Oh God" prayers, or the "If it be Thy will" prayers.

"If it be Thy will" prayers are not very effective, because we are not standing firmly in faith for anything. It is wishy-washy at best, but sounds spiritual. Ask God in prayer what His will is in a certain matter, and then pray with conviction what He has said is His will. Many times we can find His will in the Word of God. We need to get a promise in the Scripture, and then stand on it to get offensive in

> **Ask God in prayer what His will is in a certain matter, and then pray with conviction what He has said is His will.**

our prayers. It is time to stop being a defensive player and get on the offensive! When we do this it will confuse the enemy—especially if we usually play a defensive game. It is time for the Body of Christ to get on the offensive, as a player built for the battlefield. We need to press in and take territory for the pulling down of strongholds.

When we press in with courage, we break off the spirit of fear. In the final scene of the *Karate Kid* movie with Jackie Chan, the boy is injured badly because the opposing team hurt his knee on purpose. He was limping and fighting bravely and had a choice to continue or give up in the competition.

The teacher suggested that he quit, but the boy looked at his teacher and said, "I need to go out and fight."

His teacher asked him, "Why?"

The boy said, "Because I still have fear. I need to fight and stand until I am not afraid anymore."

Sometimes we are in the battle not only to win, but to conquer our fear. God wants us to fight our fear head on, and not be afraid of the enemy anymore. Pressing in leaves no room for fear to gain a foothold in our lives. The Scriptures says, "The Spirit who lives in you is greater than the spirit who lives in the world."[17] When we no longer call fear a "trusted friend," then it has no hold on us and we walk in a new-found level of authority.

In Japan, the Samurai were elite warriors who used a sword and they had great strategy. Sarah Ernst, teacher of the *Warrior Mind Training*, said the Samurai would "cultivate the elite warrior mind, spending hours and hours focusing their minds so that when it was time to go into battle, they knew how to turn off their thoughts and have razor-sharp attention. There were not any thoughts or doubts that would cause them to hesitate— especially in the most critical moments."[18]

This elite warrior mindset is true for us as believers. When we focus on God's Word with laser-like clarity, then we can turn off the chatter of the enemy. We are an undefeatable opponent to the devil when we press in, fight our fears, and trust that God has our back at all times.

The greatest moments in the Wilderness are found in the hardest of times. After we come out of the Wilderness, we realize how sweet and precious the Wilderness experience was. God builds our character not only to sustain us in the journey, but to conquer and occupy territory once we are in the Promised Land.

OUR PRAYER TO GOD

God,

Thank You for the precious gift of the Wilderness. I want to go through every stage that You have intended in order to build in me the character to sustain me in the journey. I give up the spirit of control. I give up trying to control the circumstances. I give up controlling people around me. I give up controlling even the timing in the Wilderness. I loose trust. I trust that You have my destiny in Your hand, and that my destiny is good. I trust that You have my back. Help me in the areas where I still struggle trusting You. I want to know You—not just Your works. I desire to trust You in all things and in all ways.

No longer will I play it safe or small in a defensive position, but I press in on the offensive. I bind fear and move forward despite the circumstances. I loose courage. I stand in the new-found confidence You are giving me and trust that You are ever pulling me into my destiny.

Amen

GOD'S PRAYER TO US

My Child,

I see your struggle and I know your pain. The Wilderness carries with it the lessons learned to form the character in you that I need developed to take on your Promised Land.

Press in—press in—press in. For it is in the act of pressing in that your wings are being strengthened. It is the "pressing in" that builds your strength, not necessarily in the "winning" of the battle. It is in the pressing in and standing that you will get stronger. Stand for what is right no matter the odds—no matter what the crowd says—no matter what others around you say. It is in the standing and pressing in that the victory is found, and it is a victory like no other. It is a victory of the heart. It is a deepening of character

Trust Me. I am worthy of all your trust. I know all about you because I made you. When I made you, I saw the finished product in you, and all the stages in between. I see you how you were created to be. Allow me to form you into My image through the Wilderness journey. Allow Me to pull out the character traits that are already embedded in you, for you will need them to complete the journey.

I love you and told you so by laying down everything I had at the cross. If I can lay down My all, then lay down your all. I will never leave you, nor forsake you. **I AM** *a trustworthy God!*

Love,
El Shaddai
Lord God Almighty

STUDY GUIDE

1. In your prayer time, ask God if there are any areas in your life that you still have control over—areas you have not completely surrendered to Him. As He reveals these to you, pray and release them to Him. Write them down in your journal.

2. Are there areas in your life where you have not carried your own oil? For example, you may have leaned too hard on others for prayer support, but you have not put in the necessary time in prayer or reading God's Word that you need to right now. Ask for forgiveness and begin to step up in those areas where you need to carry your own oil. Ask God what that looks like in your own life.

3. Are there areas of fear that have kept you grid-locked in your "comfort zone"? Pray and ask God what those areas may be in your life. Make a choice and begin to take a step of courage. Move out of your comfort zone.

END NOTES

1. Exodus 17:1a (NASB). Note: The phrase ends, "Wilderness of Sin." "Sin" in this context is not the Hebrew word "Chattaath", but is capitalized and represents a physical location (*Ciyn* in Hebrew). The literal translation means "the tract of wilderness between Elim and Sinai." *Strong's Exhaustive Concordance: New American Standard Bible.* Retrieved from http://www.blueletterbible.org.

2. Exodus 23:29-30 (NASB).

3. See Matthew 25.

4. Isaiah 54:2 (NIV).

5. Hebrews 10:38-39 (NASB).

6. Luke 22:42 (NASB).

7. Luke 22:43 (NASB).

8. Romans 5:4 (NLT, Emphasis added).

9. Hebrews 10:36 (NASB, Emphasis added).

10. Habakkuk 2:3 (NASB).

11. Mary Anne Radmacher.

12. Job 11:18 (NLT).

13. 2 Corinthians 10:4 (NKJV).

14. Malachi 3:10 (NASB, Emphasis added).

15. Isaiah 53:5 (NLT, Emphasis added).

16. Matthew 16:19 (NIV, Emphasis added).

17. 1 John 4:4b (NLT).

18. Sarah Ernst. *Warrior Mind Training.* Retrieved from: http://www.psmag.com/health/a-state-military-mind-42839/.

CHAPTER NINE

DELAYS IN THE WILDERNESS

"How long O Lord, until you restore me?"
Psalm 6:3b (NLT)

"How long, O Lord?" is the cry of our hearts in the Wilderness. "Have you forgotten me, Lord?" is a common question many of us ask. Even after stepping out in obedience there can be delays. Delays are common-place in the Wilderness. They are similar to the signs on the freeways that say, "Expect Delays" while they are under construction. The Wilderness is a time of construction in our lives. It is building in us the tenacity or fortitude to go the distance and are common-place.

The story of David illustrates delays. David was secretly anointed to be king, but then went back to tending his sheep. He did not step into his kingship until many years later, when he became King of Judah. Even more years went by before he became King over all of Israel.

The Lord spoke to me clearly at a low point in my Wilderness and said, "You are not forgotten in your field." This word was based on this story of David. David was faithfully tending sheep in his field when God chose him to become Saul's music leader. He was selected by his faithfulness in his field. Likewise, God has not forgotten us in our fields. Wherever we are in our Wilderness experience, God sees us. Nothing can separate us from God's love. He sees all that we are going through and truly cares. At the right time, after the delay, we will be lifted up into the proper position He has for us.

ARE WE THERE YET?

When we were children most of us heard our parents say, "Patience is a virtue." Remember how, as children, driving in a car on vacation, we asked our parents, "Are we there yet?" We kept asking them over and over, "Are we there yet? Are we there yet?" As a parent, you may be on the receiving end of this with your own children, squawking that same line. The answer was (and always is) the same, "Have patience, we are almost there." We are excited to arrive at our destination, but we need the patience it takes to get there.

The Wilderness is filled with times of impatience because we desperately want to "arrive" at the destination God has for us. Many times we ask, "Are we there yet?" or the more desperate question, "When will this *ever* end?" But this journey is a process, and along the road of construction there will be delays.

WAITING THROUGH THE DELAY

Wait means "to *rest* in expectation," while *tarry* means "to *linger* in expectation." *Delay* means "to be *slower* than expected." All of these terms are based on our *expectations*. What are we expecting? At times it feels like our expectations have been dashed against the rocks, and we are being hopelessly washed up on shore. Can we continue to trust God when our expectations seem to be unfulfilled, or come slower than anticipated? That is where our faith is formed. It is in the delays that our true character is being developed.

My friend, Deb, was going through a tough Wilderness experience and the Lord told her, "Get close to me. Take one day at a time. **Expect** Me to show up for you." God wanted her to continue to **expect** Him to show up for her. Waiting with **expectancy** is one of the keys in the delay part of journey.

205

Expectation is an attitude of the heart that still believes. This is one of the toughest things to do in the Wilderness, because circumstances are speaking so loudly to us that they can drown out God's voice. In the Wilderness, the goal of the enemy is to separate us from God. *His mission is to get us to believe that God does not love us or care about us.* This is the biggest lie of the enemy and probably the most effective one as well.

One time, when I was in prayer with a good friend who was going through the Wilderness, the Lord gave me a picture. He was cupping her cheeks with His hands and gently wiping her tears away with His thumbs as He was caressing her face. It was such a vivid picture in prayer that I began to cry because I could feel the love God had for her. It took me awhile to stop crying and express to her how much God loves her through her tough situation. So many times in church we hear, "God loves us," but when we truly experience the love of God in our Wilderness, it becomes very real and tangible.

Contrary things happen in the Wilderness. Situations come that we have not anticipated. It is not the event, per se, that is the issue. It is how we *interpret* the situation. It is the *meaning* we attach to what happened.

My friend, Deb, and her mom, Sandy, felt the Lord say to them, "Do not allow the enemy to write reality for you. Will you let **Me** define reality or will you cling to your own interpretation and assumptions? Check your assumptions at the door and let

> Do not allow the enemy to write reality for you.

Me define your reality." Circumstances are not your truth. God's Word will always be your guide and the truth in any situation.

We can see an example of this when the Israelites were scouting out the Promised Land and saw the enemy in the land. *God said*, "I promised you a good land flowing with milk and honey." But *they said*, "Why God have you brought us here to kill us?"[1] The Israelites let the enemy define their reality and they created their own assumptions about the land. God said one thing, but they put their own assumptions on the situation. We need to let God write our reality for us, and *not* the enemy.

During these delays, a spirit of disappointment can set in. We can lose hope and our expectation that God will come through for us. The story of Mary, Martha, and Lazarus is a prime example of allowing a spirit of disappointment to come. Lazarus, a friend of Jesus, got sick. His sisters, Mary and Martha, called for Jesus to come and heal Lazarus, since He had healed so many others. This was the same Mary who had anointed Jesus' feet with a year's worth of oil. She had given up ALL she had, and laid it at Jesus' feet, wiping them with her tears and hair. She was completely "sold out" to Jesus, so she thought, "Surely He will come right away to help my brother."

The *expectation* was that Jesus would immediately come to help them, but it did not happen that way. Jesus took his time getting there. When He finally showed up four days later, it was too late, Lazarus was dead. It is interesting that Scripture says Jesus loved Mary, Martha, and Lazarus. In the book of John, it takes one whole verse to make sure the reader knows that Jesus loved them![2] Yet, He was delayed in coming. When He did show up, Martha ran to meet him, but Mary sat in the house and did not come right away. Mary had a spirit of disappointment. After all that she had given Him and laid at His feet, she was disappointed that He did not come through for her in the *way she* thought He would. Jesus loved her, and did come through for her later in the story, but she had a certain *way* that she expected it to happen. *She allowed the enemy to write her reality for her!*

Martha said to Him, "Lord, if you had been here, my brother would not have died. Even now I know that whatever You ask of God, God will give You."[3] Jesus told her that Lazarus would rise again, but she thought He was talking about her brother going to heaven someday. She had one level of faith, but Jesus was about to take her to a whole new level of faith. Martha told Mary to come and see Jesus, and so she went out quickly and fell at his feet saying the same thing that Martha did. They took Jesus to Lazarus' tomb and there Jesus wept. The Jews said, "Could not this man, who opened the eyes of the blind man, have kept this man also from dying?"[4] They questioned Jesus as well. It was then Jesus called Lazarus out of the tomb and raised him from the dead.

Mary had a spirit of disappointment. Jesus had not showed up the *way* she thought He would. She believed that Jesus could heal him, but He was up to something much greater in their lives than just a healing. He was bringing resurrection power to the situation. His delay brought a spirit of disappointment because her expectations were dashed against the rocks of her despair.

Many times we feel the same way. We may have been standing on a promise that God gave us and **did** have faith to believe at one level. Our expectations were that God was going to show up, but then He did not show up the *way* we thought. We can become like Mary,[5] where we sit down in the house and do not even come out to see Jesus, because we have a spirit of disappointment. Thoughts like, "God does not love me," come to our mind constantly like the waves crashing on the shore. God **will** show up, it just may not be on our time table. That is the delay in the Wilderness. God's end goal is to bring Him even greater Glory. Raising Lazarus from the dead was even more glorious than healing him from sickness. God does love us tremendously and He **will** show up. However, there may just be a delay in the process.

Delays are also God's way of proving what is inside our hearts. What comes to the surface in delays are telltale signs of what is in our hearts. God already knows what is in our hearts, but He is letting *us* see it for ourselves.

God uses the word *wait* many times in the Bible. In the Scripture it says, "In the morning, O Lord, you hear my voice...I lay my request before you and *wait in expectation*."[6] It also says, "For the vision is yet for the appointed time; It hastens toward the goal and it will not fail. Though it *tarries*, *wait* for it; For it will certainly come, it will not *delay*.[7]

The promises God gives us may tarry or delay, but the Word says we must wait for them with an expectant heart. He is able *AND* He is willing to do that thing which He promised. Our delay is not God's bad timing. He is never late. However, when our expectations go unrealized during our waiting period because of a delay, a spirit of disappointment can come. The delay causes us to doubt our unfulfilled expectations. Stay strong in the Lord and in the power of His might. Take one day at a time and continue to believe, despite the delay.

Delays come in many forms—an expected job promotion that has appeared to have passed us by, a desire to be married with no prospects on the horizon, or a financial crisis that was supposed to have been resolved but was not. Delays can cause us to doubt whether we have heard from God correctly. We can begin to lose hope. "Did God really say this over my life?" or, "Can I really trust that God will do what He promised to me?"

The temptation for "A" type personalities is to *make it happen* ourselves, since we cannot seem to find God anywhere. For other, less stressed personalities, the temptation is to sit down and quit. What we do in our delay is a telling sign of what we believe in our hearts. It is in the delays of life we either choose to trust God, no matter what, or we try to *make something happen* in our own strength. When we try to make things happen, just to get something moving, we do it for the sake of momentum. We

> **What we do in our delay is a telling sign of what we believe in our hearts.**

act on the false belief, "Well, at least if I am moving, it feels like I am getting somewhere." This really means we are just going on another trip around the mountain! We feel like we are getting somewhere when there is momentum, however much can be accomplished by *waiting* and *resting* in the Lord with *expectancy*. The Scripture says, "Let us labor therefore to enter into that rest."[8] It sounds odd to have to labor to enter rest, but with the busyness of our lives it can be very challenging to rest. God wants us to continue to expect Him to show up. By resting, we are demonstrating our belief that He will show up and take care of us.

We have no control over the timing in the Wilderness. The Israelites were guided by God's cloud in the day and His fire by night. "They traveled and camped at the Lord's command wherever He told them to go. Then they remained in their camp as long as the cloud stayed over the Tabernacle. Whether the cloud stayed above the Tabernacle for two days, a month, or a year, the people of Israel stayed in camp and did not move on. But as soon as it lifted, they broke camp and moved on."[9] I always thought that the cloud by day and fire by night to lead them meant they traveled through the Wilderness and kept moving every day. In fact, there were periods when they camped for months or even a year at a time in a certain spot.

This is true for us as well. There may be times when we are moving, but there will be occasions when we seem to be in the same spot for months on end. This is not always easy. Truly waiting on the Lord means we only move when He moves, and we stay when He says to stay. It is learning to move in partnership with Him.

Listening is critical in order to be in effective partnership with Him. We cannot move when He says to move, or stay when He says to stay, if we are not paying attention to His voice. By continuing in prayer and reading His Word, we put ourselves in a position to hear His voice every day.

POINT A TO POINT B

In the Wilderness we do not always go the direct route, much to our chagrin. Preachers sometimes talk about the true distance in the Wilderness, from Point A at the Red Sea, to Point B at the Jordan Crossing. It should have taken only eleven days to complete this trip. While this is true as the crow flies, God did not take them the straight route. He took them to what seemed like a dead end—the Red Sea.

By looking at a map of their position, you can see there was a way the children of Israel could have gotten to the other side without crossing the Red Sea. However, this was not the way God took them. He did not give them the short cut. *He sent them in the direction that would best show off His glory.* By taking them through the Red Sea, the Israelites saw such a huge miracle which, even the people of Jericho were still talking about it forty years later. With their backs against the Red Sea and no possible escape, God ensured there was no doubt about His power (and glory) by having them cross on dry land.

It is the same in our lives. God may lead us to what appears to be a dead end and we can get frustrated because we could have gone a shorter way. But God did not lead us that way. He wants to lead us to the way that best shows off His glory for years to come.

There are many stories illustrating this in the Bible. Look at Daniel in the lion's den, Joseph in jail, or Esther, when her enemies wanted to kill all the Jews. Each time, it seemed like *God* led the person to a dead end, but it was all about showing off His glory. What God did in Egypt was remembered by the people in Jericho forty years later! It had lasting impact and staying power for the glory of God.

When we hit what looks like a dead end, it is actually an end to ourselves. It is an end to the spirit of control. It is an end to a season or era in our lives that needs to be jettisoned in order to begin the new thing God is doing. A new beginning needs

When we hit what looks like a dead end, it is actually an end to ourselves.

to start with a clear ending. We can get nostalgic over what was and think it was so much better, but God is leading us to a new thing. We are becoming new wine in a new wine skin. We have a new way of thinking, a new way of behaving, and a new way of doing things. Doing everything the way we have always done it will not work in this new season. We have to change in order to move through the Wilderness. We need to be open to this season we are entering. We have to give up control and let the Lord lead and guide us, even if does not seem like the right, or quickest way to go from Point A to Point B.

When the children of Israel went through the Red Sea, God still did not take them the direct route. When they wanted to take the shortest route through Edom, the people of that country said, "No!" In the Bible, I do not see God taking many people on the short straight route. There are many times when He took them around and around the mountain.

One day I told God, "I do not want to go around this mountain one more time." He reminded me of the story of the potter's wheel. As the wheel spins, the clay goes around and around. With each pass new things are being fashioned in the clay. It is slowly being shaped with each cycle to become what it was created to be. When God molds us and forms us into the vessel that He wants, we may well need to go around and around the mountain until we are fully equipped for His service in the next season of our lives.

AROUND THIS MOUNTAIN ONE MORE TIME

When we go around and around the mountain, taking laps, God is actually instilling in us patience, fortitude, and an impartation of His Spirit. We need to change in order to fit through the next door He is opening. A mantle, like a needed covering, will come for *the work* that He has called us to do. In the New Testament, we see Paul and Barnabas set apart for *the work* to which God set them. They were already doing the work, but now they were set apart for the *new work* into which they were entering. So too, we need to be set apart for this new work that God wants to do in us. By waiting on Him, we will receive what we need in this next season. By standing still through the delay we will see the full manifestation of the direction He wants to lead us. Linger in His presence and let the covering of a new mantle fall and the anointing will come.

TIMING IN THE WILDERNESS

One time during her Wilderness journey, my friend prayed a gutsy prayer. She said, "God, I will be here in this Wilderness for as long as it takes to make me into what You want me to be." To be honest, I was not praying for that in my Wilderness journey. My goal was to get out as fast as I could, because it was the toughest thing I had ever gone through. For a long time I mistakenly thought, "If I am a super good Christian and do everything perfect in this Wilderness, then I will get out of here really fast, and move on to the next thing God has for me. If I am a *good* servant, then my time in the Wilderness will be short." It was almost as if I was looking at time in the Wilderness as a jail sentence. This is untrue. This perception is based on our works.

The fallacy is this, "If I work hard enough, I can get myself out." The fact is that the Wilderness is a process (or what I have been referring to as a *process event*), and we must go through it in its entirety to receive all that is supposed to be accomplished. We cannot speed up the process by being **good**. A friend once told me, "Let time have time." Time is the natural equalizer that produces in us patience and endurance for the race that is set before us.

I remember as a child, while attending summer camp, walking to an area called "the Cove." It was a steep uphill climb for at least two miles. As an adult I went back to the same place and rode my bike. I was surprised. It was not as tough as I remembered. My endurance had been built up to such a point that what *was* once hard in my youth was *now* easy in my maturity.

As we continue to be faithful and obedient to what God is calling us to, we will begin to see that trials have a purpose and mold in us the strength of character we need to handle the journey. There will be stops along the way—character building stops, uncomfortable stops. But God truly *is good* and we can trust Him to come through for us because He is always on time.

DELAYED GRATIFICATION

During the Wilderness I needed *hope* for the future so badly that I kept looking for a "consolation prize" for giving up those things that were very dear to me while in the Wilderness. There are no "consolation prizes" for being in the Wilderness, however, there are tremendous gifts that are imparted to us as we journey through. We may not realize they are gifts until we have come out and are on the other side. I remember thinking, "If I do this "X" thing, God, will you at least give me this "Y" thing?"

There is no bargaining in the Wilderness. We must be willing to say, "God, I will obey, even if it means I put everything on the altar and give it all up not knowing what will happen." It is a complete surrender and trust that God is good and He truly does love us and will take care of us. This is a tough lesson to learn, but one that has tremendous impact later.

ALL DELAYS ARE NOT GOD'S DELAYS

Israel sent messengers to the king of the Amorites asking them to let them pass through their land, but they said no just like the Edomites who had refused them passage through their land earlier.[10] This time Israel fought them, won the battle, and crossed through their land.[11]

Just because we encounter a detour the first time does not mean we will never need to hit a situation "head on" the next time around. No longer on the defensive, the Israelites crossed over the Jordan and launched an offensive attack.

The key is to ask God whether this delay is from Him, or if is it from the enemy; if so, we need to take up our sword and fight. Only God knows the encounters we will face in the Wilderness.

There are many examples of wrong choices the Israelites made while they were delayed—from complaining, to taking matters into their own hands, to building a false idol.

COMPLAINING IN THE DELAY

The Children of Israel "Set out from Mount Hor by the way of the Red Sea, to go around the land of Edom; and the people became *impatient* (or *disappointed*) because of the journey. The people spoke against God and Moses, 'Why have you brought us up out of Egypt to die in the Wilderness? For there is no food, and no water, and we loathe this miserable food.' And the Lord sent fiery serpents among the people and they bit the people, so that many people of Israel died. 'We have sinned, because we have spoken against the Lord and you; intercede with the Lord, that He may remove the serpents from us. And Moses interceded for the people.'"[12]

The children of Israel complained because of the delay in the Wilderness. We are also tempted to become impatient and complain. God did not send the fiery serpents in the Wilderness. The serpents were *there* in the Wilderness from the very start of their journey, but God had a hedge of protection over the Israelites so that they would not get bitten. The Scripture says, "Whoso breaketh a hedge, a serpent shall bite him."[13] By complaining and not wanting to go the long way, the people broke the hedge of protection God had established around them.

> **Complaining is one way to break down a hedge of protection God has placed around us in the Wilderness.**

Complaining is one way to break down a hedge of protection God has placed around us.

There are things which allow the hedge of God to come down.

For example, when we use words like *always* and *never.* This is a telling sign that we are in the complaining zone.

In this story, God had Moses set up a bronze serpent[14] as a type and shadow of looking to Christ when we get bitten by the enemy. A serpent on a pole is the symbol for our medical community today, drawn from this story in the Bible. God is our healer in all areas of our lives. God did not take away the snakes. He gave the Israelites a way of escape from death by looking to the bronze snake.

In our problems, when we spend time with God and look to Him, our problems may not go away, but we are different from just a gaze into the face of Jesus. The *situation* may not be different, but *we* are different coming out of the situation. We come out with a new mind-set which is the driving force that changes the circumstances we are in. The best anti-venom for complaining is a thankful heart.

DELAYS THAT BIRTH A GOLDEN CALF

Another delay came when Moses went up to the mountain to get the Ten Commandments. He took longer than the people expected. When God takes longer than expected, we become tempted to take matters into our own hands. We want to "help"

221

God get this thing going. The Wilderness was tough enough to handle, then Moses disappeared for forty days. This was a delay within the delay.

When the delay hits another delay, bitterness or self-pity may begin to creep in. A feeling of, "Others are blessed, why not me?" whispers discontentment to us. The temptation is to take things into our own hands and *do* something! We may race out to find any old job or pursue a new relationship instead of waiting on God through the delay to find out what He is doing. In a way, we are subconsciously trying to force God's hand to move when the delay is part of His process.

With Moses gone, the children of Israel created a replacement for God. They built a golden calf. The children of Israel gave up their gold earrings as an offering to make the golden calf. With the work of their own hands they made the idol, and then offered sacrifices to it. "When the people (Israelites) saw that Moses delayed to come down from the mountain, the people assembled about Aaron and said to him, 'Come, make us a god who will go before us; as for this Moses, the man who brought us up from the land of Egypt, we do not know what has become of him.' And Aaron said to them, 'Tear off the gold rings which are in the ears of your wives, your sons, and your daughters, and bring them to me.'"[15]

It is interesting that they took off the gold rings that were attached to their ears. In Egypt, the gold rings in their ears symbolized their enslavement. Thus, they exchanged one form of slavery for another, and made a golden calf.

There will be seasons of delay in the Wilderness. Times when it seems like God is not listening and is nowhere to be found. At times God *steps back* to watch and see what we are going to do. Are we going to continue trusting Him, or will we take back control and try to *make something happen* just for the sake of momentum? It is easy to judge the Children of Israel and think it was silly to make a golden calf. But how many times have we made our own personal "golden calf" and offered sacrifices to it? We may have built our own business without the Lord, and then offered a sacrifice of time or money to it. Or, we may have used food as a way to comfort ourselves (and lifted it to a higher position) instead of going to the Lord. One way to know if we have a "golden calf" in our lives is to consider what our resources are being poured into. Are we giving power to the thing we built with our own hands? Are we sacrificing our family, time, or money to one thing we want to keep that God has told us to release? What holds our attention more than the Lord? What does God want us to release in the Wilderness that we are still hanging on to?

223

We need to release the things God has said we need to release, whether they are people, material items, or something else.

> We need to release the things God has said we need to release.

In all likelihood this will be tremendously hard to do, but it is a sacrificial offering to the Lord. If we have birthed a golden calf, we can repent and give to God an offering.

Just before the golden calf affair, God was speaking to Moses about a man named Bezalel. Bezalel was a master craftsman. God had filled him with the Spirit in wisdom, in understanding, in knowledge, and in all kinds of craftsmanship to make artistic designs for work in gold, silver, and bronze. God had imparted this gift to Bezalel to work with gold and fashion the important furnishings for the Tabernacle.[16] The very same gift that can be used for God's glory can also be used for the enemy. Since our gifts and talents are irrevocable, our gifts need to be refined in the Wilderness so that what comes out of us is for God's glory.

DELAYS THAT BIRTH AN ISHMAEL

Abraham had a promise from God that his descendents would be numbered like the sand of the sea.[17] Abraham and Sarah waited twenty-five years for a child, but Sarah was barren the whole time. Sarah grew impatient in her delay and took matters into her own hands. Nothing seemed to be happening in the natural. Her biological clock was ticking. Actually, it had stopped ticking many years prior! Can you really blame her? After ten years of waiting she decided to talk Abraham into having a son with her maidservant. Abraham listened to his wife to make her happy. This was Abraham and Sarah's own personal delay in the Wilderness. The maidservant conceived and bore a son named Ishmael.[18]

Abraham then *lifted up* Ishmael (as his own golden calf) and asked God to *bless it*. Abraham asked God to bless what *he* had created. God said I will bless your Ishmael, but that is not my will for you. Because you asked I will bless him, but I am still going to do My will and send you a Son of the Promise named Isaac.[19]

Beware of "birthing an Ishmael" while in delay, and then with your own *mouth* asking God to bless it. God may honor your request and bless the very thing that He did not intend to bring about in your life, but there will be consequences to it. Many times I have stepped out in my own flesh, especially in business, and then asked God to bless business deals that He did not lead me to in the first place. Blessing Ishmael had consequences. The maidservant now despised Sarah and there was a feud between them. Sarah eventually kicked out both the maidservant and

Ishmael and sent them away. Abraham was heartbroken (after all this was his son too!) The thing he birthed with his own hands was now being banished.

Waiting on the Lord through the delay is important. We need to be very careful what we ask God to bless in the Wilderness, and that it is not something we birthed in our own accord. He is aligning and preparing not only us, but others who will be affected by our calling. It is like a stop light. If it is red, stop! If we plow through a red light, we should not be surprised if we are hit by an oncoming car. Can we fix the car and go to physical therapy when it is all over? Sure. But there will be a lot of pain and anguish we can save ourselves from if we will just stop!

PUSH THROUGH THE ENEMIES DELAY

I went rock climbing and reppelling in one of our national forests. When I reached the top of one of the peaks, I discovered there were two rock faces. I could choose to rappel down either one. I asked my guide which was the toughest route and he said, "The one on the right." So, off I went to the right. The drop was only eighty feet, but it looked like 1,000 feet, because of the perspective of the horizon. We were on top of a cliff and we could see the whole valley below us. We could also see the mountains in the distance, so it seemed higher than it was.

For me, the toughest part of rappelling is getting my initial footing and stepping out onto the ledge. I have to lean back as far as I can and trust the ropes to hold me completely on their own.

Once I lean back, everything else is fun, and I go whizzing down the side of the rock face. I did it once with no trouble and had a blast. So, I decided to go again.

The right side was the toughest route on the rock face because it had a huge outcropping forcing you hang nearly upside down. You have to push off with your feet and hit the underside of the rock. This time when I pushed off, I hit the rock at an angle and my left ankle popped. Not a good thing to hear when you are eighty feet off the ground! I had to assess how hurt I was. The shooting pain in my ankle mixed with the adrenaline rush made me sick to my stomach. So there I was dangling over a cliff face, twenty feet down with sixty feet more to go, trying to figure out if I could make it the rest of the way down, plus I *still* had the climb out of the canyon.

I decided to go for it. (Did I really have a choice?) I figured that since I had adrenaline flowing in my body, I would be able to hike out right away.

That is how many of us feel in the Wilderness. It has taken every inch of our faith to step out onto the face of the cliff to begin our descent, to trust that God has us on belay (a term meaning holding the ropes below). Then part of the way through we are hit with a delay, some sort of harsh circumstance, and we are dangling in mid-air with a long way to go before we get down. God has us on belay, but we need to trust Him. He will not let go of the rope!

When we move in what God has for us we will be challenged to the very *core* of who we are. For some people, it will be their health. For others, it will be their home or family. Yet for others, it will be in their work or business. Each weapon that is formed against us is specifically designed to defeat us and disrupt our destiny. Each also has something to do with our destiny and what we are suppose to accomplish.

> **The enemy will attack and attempt to delay each of us in the area in which we are called.**

The enemy will attack and attempt to delay each of us in the area in which we are called. Resistance is not fun and can be very hard. However, resistance is a good thing. In order for a plane to take flight, it needs momentum. It also needs resistance, which causes air flow over the wings. This is what gives lift to an airplane, and so it is in our Spiritual life. We need to continue to move forward and when we get the *pushback* (or opposition) from the enemy it will give us the resistance we need to propel us to new heights. We are like an eagle whose wings are getting strengthened to make the journey to the top of the mountain. For every *pushback* that we encounter, we receive greater strength in our wings as we apply our faith. Then when the time is right, God will release us to soar into our destiny and what He created us to be.

OUR PRAYER TO GOD

God,

Forgive me for the times I took matters into my own hands and tried to "make things happen" just for the sake of momentum. As hard as this is, I will be here in the Wilderness for as long as it takes until You have accomplished ALL You have for me in this Wilderness. Thank You that You are at work in me, both to will and work for Your good pleasure. Thank You for producing in me patience and fortitude through the delays. Help me to draw close to You each day. Help me take one day at a time and expect You to show up for me every day. I bind the spirit of disappointment, and I loose faith in my life. I pray for a healing of the disappointments of the past when I felt like You did not come through for me. I release those negative experiences and the hurtful thoughts that came with that situation, and pray for a release of your peace and rest over my circumstances. I give You this time in the Wilderness delay and say, "Have Your way."

Amen

GOD'S PRAYER TO US

My Child,

You have been around and around this mountain before. **You have not missed Me!** *There is no way you can miss Me. I have not been in the wind, fire, or earthquake, but I am in the gentle whisper. Continue to listen for Me in that still small voice to lead and guide you. Come into My rest with great expectancy, for*

I have great plans for you. Do not become impatient if things are not the way you planned. For My plans are far greater than yours, and I always see the forest through the trees. I am the lifter of your head, and when you get through this Wilderness time, I will lift you to greater heights where you will be able to see and understand all that I have been doing. I will speak to you.

Stay in that place of rest. Stay in that place of peace, and you will hear my voice. I am grooming you to take your proper place as a Child of the Most High. I love you. Stay in My presence with quiet expectancy and you will see all that I have promised you come to pass.

Love,
El Olam
The Everlasting God

STUDY GUIDE

1. Pray and ask God if there are any areas where you are allowing the enemy to "write reality for you"? You may be putting an interpretation on a situation that is totally mistaken and is not what the Lord is intending. Ask God for His reality in your circumstances. Begin to declare His reality over your circumstances every day.

2. Have there been any delays in your Wilderness? One of the best things you can do is "sow a seed" of encouragement to someone else who is going through a Wilderness time. Write them a note, give them a call, or send them a Scripture verse to encourage them. Not only does it bring you psychological help, but you will also reap what you sow, and soon someone else will be encouraging you.

3. Pray and ask God to reveal the things He is imparting to you in the delays. It could be patience, endurance, or a host of other character traits. Write them down in your journal.

ENDNOTES

1. See Numbers 14:1-3.
2. See John 11:5.
3. John 11:21b-22 (NASB).
4. John 11:37b (NASB).
5. See John 11:20b.
6. Psalm 5:3 (NIV, Emphasis added).
7. Habakkuk 2:3 (NASB, Emphasis added).
8. Hebrews 4:11a (KJV).
9. Numbers 9:18, 22 (NLT).
10. See Numbers 20:14-20.
11. See Numbers 21:21-26.
12. Numbers 21:4-7 (NASB, Emphasis added).
13. Ecclesiastes 10:8b (KJV).
14. See Numbers 21:8-9.
15. Exodus 32:1-2 (NASB, Emphasis added).
16. See Exodus 31:2-5.
17. See Genesis 13:16.
18. See Genesis 16:1-4.
19. See Genesis 17:18-21.

CHAPTER TEN

FAITH FOR THE JOURNEY OUT

"The Lord will guide you continually,
And satisfy your soul in drought."
Isaiah 58:11a (NKJV)

"I feel like there is a big target on my back," one of my friends said of her Wilderness experience. "I am getting pummeled by the enemy. What is going on?" Many of us feel that way in the Wilderness. We feel like we are getting knocked down and when we try to get back up, we are knocked to the ground once more by some unexpected situation. Hearing from God and standing in faith both play an important role during this constant barrage of unexpected attacks. The Bible talks about different ways God can speak to us, especially during these challenging times. One of the ways is called a *"Logos"* word, which refers to the written Word of the Bible. Another is called a *"Rhema"* word, which refers to the Word of God coming alive in our spirit, or the Holy Spirit speaking to us. Both are extremely important. The Scripture says, "So then faith (comes) by hearing, and hearing by the (*Rhema*) word of God"[1] The word *hearing* in this verse is in the present tense. It is a *now* word. Something that we need from the Lord right *now!*

In the Wilderness, **both** the *Logos* word and the *Rhema* word are important. It is far easier to go through all the things we are enduring when we are hearing from the Lord—especially

> In the Wilderness, both the Logos word and the Rhema word are important.

when we are hearing things that we need *now!* It is harder to continue the journey if we do not hear from the Lord; when it seems like He is silent. The Bible says, "My sheep hear My voice, and I know them, and they follow Me."[2] We can hear God's voice every day and feel His presence even in our Wilderness times.

I grew up in a church that said they believed in the Holy Spirit and gave lip service to the Him, but basically denied the *power* of the Holy Spirit. They believed that the Holy Spirit was moving only when the disciples were doing great miracles, but somehow He became antiquated. They believed that the Holy Spirit did not move the same way today as He had done in the past. The Bible says, "Jesus Christ is the same yesterday and today and forever."[3] Jesus also said, "I tell you the truth, anyone who believes in me will do the same works I have done, and even greater works, because I am going to be with the Father."[4] Jesus went to the Father and sent us the Holy Spirit. Jesus did not put a time limit on the Holy Spirit, or say that His activity "expired" at a certain point in history.

Because I grew up with this view of the Holy Spirit, I was always "afraid" of Him. I thought those people who believed in Him were a bit crazy, and I did not want to be crazy like that. What I have come to realize is that Jesus left us the Holy Spirit as a *comforter,* and He is also our *counselor.* These are two extremely important things we need in the Wilderness. The Holy Spirit is there to *comfort* us when we feel beaten down, and He *counsels* us in the right direction. This is exactly what we need when we are going through the Wilderness.

Later in my life, I went to another church where the Pastor would open up the Sunday service with a prayer, "Speak, Lord, for your servant is listening." That used to freak me out! I would be sitting in church with my mind racing 100 miles an hour saying, "Are you going to speak to me God? What are you going to say? I do not hear anything. Oh no! Am I not as good as others in church?" On and on the chatter went through my mind. I was so flipped out and scared that for many years I did not fully embrace the Holy Spirit and the power that He could bring to my life.

Once, at the beginning of the New Year, I declared it to be "The Year of the Holy Spirit" in my life. I said I was open to what He wanted to do in my heart, and I wanted more of Him. I have been hearing from God consistently. A constant flow of impressions, words, and concrete things that I hear stream through my heart. I have received so many impressions that many times I say, "God, is that really you, or did I just make that up in my head?"

My friend, Deb, gave me a great piece of advice that has helped me with thoughts like this. She said, "Whenever you get an impression from the Holy Spirit in your heart, ask God for the corresponding Scripture in the Bible to confirm what you heard." When I tried this for the very first time, I asked God to confirm what I was sensing, and right away a verse came to me that went with the impression I felt. It was amazing! I wish someone would have shared this with me a long time ago about the power of the Holy Spirit, and how we can confirm those impressions with verses from the Bible.

When we hear from God our faith is increased. We get the encouragement we need to keep going and not lose hope while we are in the Wilderness. The Bible says, "Hope does not disappoint, because the love of God has been poured out within our hearts through the Holy Spirit who was given to us."[5] I would encourage you to ask the Holy Spirit to become more a part of your life, and open up to allow Him to be your counselor and comforter during this tough time in the Wilderness. He also comes with power and authority that will transform your life.

One of the many purposes of the Wilderness is to shift old ways of thinking and bring us to a higher level. It is also called *transition*. Lance Wallnau, a transformational trainer said, "Transition is feeling like you are going through hell, but you know God is in it!" I cannot think of a more appropriate definition of how we can feel in the Wilderness. God is using transition to shift us out of wrong thinking and to release a greater dimension in our faith. Sometimes God uses things in the natural to remind us of the shift He is doing, and to activate our faith. I call those *Faith Releasers*.

FAITH RELEASERS

Faith Releasers come into our lives to activate the faith that is already inside of us to help it grow. Communion, baptism, and fasting are some foundational *Faith Releasers*. We can take communion at home and it is a reminder about what Jesus has done for us, but it also can be a *Faith Releaser* for health and healing. I have many friends who take communion on a regular basis to release their faith for physical healing. Baptism displays our faith in a public way that we have chosen Jesus as our Savior. It is a covenant seal with God and marks a tangible moment when we accepted His forgiveness—an acknowledgement that our sins are forever washed away. Fasting also acts as a *Faith Releaser* when important decisions need to be made. These are foundational type *Faith Releasers*, but there are unconventional types of *Faith Releasers* as well.

One day when I really needed encouragement in the area of finances, I heard a traveling evangelist share his testimony. He travels with his family 300 days out of the year and told us how God had financially provided for them. He told story after story of God's goodness and God's provision. It was not just a *teaching.* It was an impartation and a *Faith Releaser.* I came away from that meeting encouraged—what God could do for one man, He could do for me. God can use anything that gives momentum to our faith as a *Faith Releaser.* There are also *Faith Releasers* God brings to us in the most humorous sort of way.

PENNIES FROM HEAVEN

One time I was praying about a situation in my company where clients were not paying invoices they owed. I kept praying, "Not a penny would fall to the ground that is due to me. Not a penny, not a penny, not a penny." I could not stop praying this prayer.

Even though I wanted to stop, I could *NOT* stop! I repeated this same line over and over for a good twenty minutes until I felt released to stop praying. Since that day, God uses pennies to change my old ways of thinking about finances, and to shift my mind-set about money. It has become a *Faith Releaser* in my life. Whenever I am worried about finances, I will find a penny. I find pennies in the most unusual places. Sometimes I find them on the ground right outside my car door, or in the middle of the rug in the house.

One time I was at a fancy performance and concerned about the high prices at the event. (Fifteen dollars for a hot dog can be a bit daunting.) I sat next to a lady and struck up a conversation. I introduced myself to her and practically fell out of my seat when she turned to me, shook my hand, and said, "Hello, my name is Penny." If anyone says God does not have a sense of humor I do not believe them. This was God's way of showing me not to worry about the high prices of the event, but instead to enjoy the company of my daughter who I brought with me, which was the *more* important thing.

I told this story about pennies to one of my friends. She told God that she did not like pennies, but would like dimes to remind her of His faithfulness in her Wilderness experience. You guessed it. Whenever she needs encouragement she now finds dimes.

241

If we will stay open to seeing them, God will use *Faith Releasers* to help shift old mind-sets that need to be changed. It may be a shift away from a poverty mentality, self-pity, depression, or a host of other mind-sets that do not line up with who we are in Christ.

One example of a *Faith Releaser* in the Bible is when Paul anointed handkerchiefs and passed them out to people. When people received one, they would be instantly healed. The handkerchief itself did not have any special magical power, but it was a "touch point" to release that person's faith. Another example is the woman with the issue of blood in the Bible. She believed in her heart that if she could touch the hem of Jesus' garment she would be healed. Her faith was in touching His garment. There was no magical quality in His garment. Many people touched Him. But she believed, and because of that it released her faith to be healed. She had to press in despite the crowd. Her *faith drove her* to see the manifestation of what she believed for, and therefore she got her healing.

Her faith drove her and therefore she got her healing.

Faith touches the heart of God. In the Old Testament many times God had the Children of Israel place remembrance stones at certain locations. The stones were to be a memorial to what the Lord had done. Passover is a good example of the next generation rehearsing all that God had done for their parents coming out of Egypt. It was a *Faith Releaser* for them and their children. When we create *Faith Releasers* or set up remembrance stones, it is a way for us to continue to believe God for big things, and it helps release hope and faith. Too many times we hear people telling us to not get our hopes up, but that is *small thinking*. God is big. He wants us to begin to believe for unfeasible things that He wants to impart to us. God is the God of impossibilities. Jesus could not perform miracles in His own home town because of unbelief. He required the people to have faith released in order for Him to show up in a big way with signs and wonders. Today we need to believe God for big things. It is important to get are hopes up and set up remembrance stones and markers along the way.

We can create remembrance stones (or *Faith Releasers*) in our lives today in a variety of creative ways. If we are standing in faith for something or a promise that God has given us, we could cut out a picture that represents that promise and post it on a bulletin board.

I know a woman who released her faith for a baby and began to buy baby clothes before she was even pregnant. Another way to release faith is to write down some Scriptures God has given us, and put them on our refrigerator. The ideas are endless. *Faith Releasers* will redirect our old ways of thinking that are not healthy, and aid us in shifting to new mind-sets.

God wants to take us to a level of greatness in His Kingdom, but we need to start by coming out of old mind-sets that not only put *us* in a box, but put *God* in a box as well. It is time to think big, act big, and go big. There is a saying in card games, "Play big or go home." I believe God is telling us the same thing in these last days. Play big or go home. God is big and He wants us to go big as well. There is only one way to please God and that is through faith. "Without faith it is impossible to please God, because anyone who comes to him must believe that He exists and that He rewards those who earnestly seek Him."[6]

What are we standing in faith for? Is it a good parking spot at church or for a nation? *Going big* is not only believing God can do great things, but that He wants *us* to be a part of the greatness that He is *about* to do. He has given to each of us a level of greatness to achieve something for Him in our lifetime. So the challenge is to ask God what mind-sets are holding us back. *It is important to ask Him what mind-sets are keeping us limited in our thinking for the destiny He has for our lives.* Then simply obey and ask Him to send a *Faith Releaser.* It will be something unique and will serve as a special encouragement to keep thinking big, and to have the faith to cross over into our own personal Promised Land.

FAITH DETERRENTS

Unbelief is a powerful foe that must be fought daily in the Wilderness. The Bible says, "So we see that they could not enter in (the *Promised Land*) because of unbelief."[7]

Unbelief is a choice. Just as *Faith Releasers* are important, we must stand our guard against *Faith Deterrents*. *Faith Deterrents* serve to bring down our faith and keep us confined in a small space. The enemy wants to knock us out, but if that will not work then keeping us contained is the next best option.

Faith Deterrents come in many different forms; from people speaking things into our lives—to our own unhealthy thoughts. We need to watch and beware of who we allow into our lives and most of all, be careful of what we allow them to speak into our lives. "Death and life are in the power of the tongue."[8] It can be *our* tongue or the tongue of *another*.

One example is someone telling us that we will never get out of debt, or that the economy is so bad we will never find a job. A *Faith Deterrent* could also be something we tell ourselves, either consciously or unconsciously, that does not line up with the Word of God. For example, someone may give a wonderful testimony of how God healed them and our response internally is to discount it and say, "It is great that God healed *them* but God will never heal *me*." This type of thinking deters and sabotages faith.

Joshua and Caleb stood in faith when they spied out the Promised Land and wanted to release faith to the other Israelites to stand on God's Promise. But the other spies sent out a *Faith Deterrent* to the Children of Israel by talking about the insurmountable enemy. The Children of Israel had to decide if they would allow their faith to be released. It was a matter of choice in who they believed. Were they going to believe Joshua and Caleb or the other spies? Joshua and Caleb talked about the huge fruit (*Faith Releaser*), and the other spies talked about the huge enemy (*Faith Deterrent*). *Faith Releasers* will always focus us on the Lord, while *Faith Deterrents* will always focus us on the enemy. In our lives there will be *Faith Releasers* and *Faith Deterrents*. Which report will we believe?

FAITH AND HOPE

"Now faith is the assurance of things **hoped** for, the conviction of things not seen."[9] Faith rests on hope. *Hope* is the emotional state which promotes the belief in a positive outcome related to circumstances in one's life. *Despair* is the opposite of hope. Many people talk about faith, but few talk about hope. If people do talk about hope it is usually in an extremely weak manner, such as "Gee, I hope we get that thing we are praying about." Hope is extremely important and is the basis of faith. Faith is the assurance of things *hoped* for. We cannot have faith without a solid foundation of hope. The definition of hope is to have a **confident expectation** that what you believe will happen or come to pass. It is not a wishy-washy hope, but a rock solid *confident expectation.*

> **Hope is to have a confident expectation that what you believe will happen or come to pass.**

Spend any length of time in the Wilderness and we may experience a sense of hopelessness. We may say to ourselves, "When is this ever going to end?" Abraham waited twenty-five years to receive his promised son, Isaac. I cannot imagine waiting twenty-five years and not wavering in faith. No wonder he is called the Father of our Faith. God reckoned Abraham's faith as righteousness. Our challenge in the Wilderness is to continue in hope and faith without wavering on the promises that God has given us. "Without faith it is impossible to please God, because anyone who comes to Him must believe that He exists and that He rewards those who *earnestly seek Him*"[10] Without hope we can have no faith, so hope becomes the foundation on which to build our faith. The Bible says, "There is surely a future hope for you, and your hope will not be cut off."[11] It also says, "For I know the plans I have for you, declares the Lord, plans to prosper you and not to harm you, plans to give you *hope* and a future."[12] "What, then, shall we say in response to this? If God is for us, who can be against us?"[13]

Sometimes we can lose hope and then make up a seemingly "godly" answer as to why the Lord did not come through for us like we thought He would. Our answers may sound spiritual, but deep down inside there is a feeling of deep *discouragement, disappointment,* and *hopelessness* that He has forgotten about us, and He is not going to come through for us. If this continues for an extended period of time it can create a "Wilderness Stronghold." According to Ed Silvoso, an evangelist, a *stronghold* is a "mind-set impregnated with hopelessness that forces you to accept as unchangeable, situations that you know are contrary to the will of God." This is similar to when a prisoner of war has been locked up for many years. It is called *Prisoner of War Syndrome.* It is characterized by withdrawal and apathy as a reaction to capture, imprisonment, and *hopelessness* about reunion with one's loved ones."[14] If we have been in the Wilderness for any extended length of time, we may get this same *Prisoner of War Syndrome,* or *Wilderness Stronghold.* We may withdraw from those around us and become apathetic towards the enemy. We can begin to see our situation as hopeless and that it will never change. This is completely false and the enemy lulls us into a pattern of acceptance, apathy, and indifference to fighting the good fight of faith. If we continue to focus on our problems in the Wilderness we miss the solutions God wants to bring to us.

We may feel the need to make up an excuse for God not coming through for us so that "we do not make Him look bad" to those around us. For example, we may believe for a new job, and when we do not find one right away we may say, "God just wants to teach me a lesson at the old job," or "God does not want me to be tempted with more money at a new job." We come up with an excuse (a way to rationalize) as to why something did not happen that we are standing in faith for, but all the while God is at work behind the scenes working all things together for our good. "For My thoughts are not your thoughts, neither are your ways My ways, declares the Lord."[15] God has the bigger picture in mind. If things do not line up on our timetable, God has not forgotten us. His ways are not our ways, plain and simple. God is big enough that we do not have to come up with justifications or excuses as to why something did not happen the way we expected.

> **If things do not line up on our timetable, God has not forgotten us.**

Our job is to continue to trust Him in unwavering hope and faith until we see this thing through.

My friend, Katherine, did not make up any excuses for God and her lack of a job. She stayed in unwavering hope and faith that God would come through for her and He did. She shares, "During a specific time in my Wilderness, I needed a job. It had taken weeks to acquire an interview. The money was dwindling and no prospective interviews were in sight. Then it hit me. It was God who led me to California. I knew then that it was God's job—not mine—to provide. I was obedient to His direction and trusted He would do His part in opening the door for me. Then I said, 'I give it to You, Lord! I take my hands completely off of it, and I know You will provide for me!' Whoo hoo! I was excited. *It was like I was running toward the edge of a cliff, knowingly; but the closer I got to the edge, the more relaxed I got.*

The very next week, five interviews suddenly appeared out of nowhere, and one of them produced a lucrative job for me—a job I am still reaping the benefits from today. I look back on that experience and realize that it was an opportunity to learn what part is my responsibility and what part is God's responsibility. I had to choose to take my hand off of what is God's responsibility—to believe He would do what He promised, and it has made all the difference!"

Abraham is a great example of faith. Even when there was no reason to hope, Abraham kept hoping—believing that he would become the father of many nations. For God had said to him, "Look at the grains of the sand. That is how many descendants you will have!" And Abraham's *faith did not weaken*, even though, at about 100 years of age, he figured his body was as good as dead, and so was Sarah's womb. "Abraham never wavered in believing God's promise. In fact, his *faith grew stronger*, and in this he brought *glory to God*. He was *fully convinced* that God was able to do whatever He promises."[16] Not only did Abraham have the hope and confident expectation that God was going to do what He promised, but his faith grew stronger as time went on. Abraham stood on God's truth and His promises to him. Usually as time goes by, we can doubt that we even heard God correctly, but Abraham's faith grew stronger and the Scripture says that this brought God glory.

It is critical to rehearse God's Truth every day and, more than once a day depending on how heavy the battle is raging.

- *The Truth is...*"No good thing does He withhold from those whose walk is blameless."[17]

- *The Truth is...* "God is bringing you into a good land."[18]

- *The Truth is*…God has "plans to prosper you…to give you hope and a future."[19]

Those are the types of *Truths* we can meditate on and speak over ourselves every day as declarations, even if our feelings do not yet match our words. Nathan Bean, a young adult pastor said, "It is not the power of your location, but the power of your declaration." We can have full assurance God is for us and He will come through even if the circumstances look completely the opposite.

When Mary and Martha called on Jesus to come and heal their brother Lazarus, He took so long that Lazarus died. When God takes His time answering us, it may be that there are things in our lives that need to die. There may be wrong mind-sets, unhealthy behaviors, or generational ways of doing things that do not benefit us and need to die in our lives before He resurrects them into something absolutely in line with our destiny. Our job is to continue to trust God and to keep our hope alive so we can have the faith to make it through. If the vision "tarries, wait for it; For it will certainly come, it will not delay"[20]

252

HOPE INSTILLED

God wants to restore hopes that have been dashed, and give us the faith we need to continue our journey out of the Wilderness. There is a story in the Bible when Elisha spoke to a Shunammite woman and asked her if she wanted a son, because he saw that she was barren. She told the man of God not to get her *hopes* up! She had long given up on having a child because her husband was old and she did not want to go down that painful road of hoping for a child and being disappointed again. Elisha prayed for her and she conceived and later gave birth to a son.

One day when her child was older, he went to his dad, said that his head hurt, and ended up dying. The woman ran to Elijah and the FIRST thing out of her mouth when she saw him was, "Did I ask you for a son? Did I tell you to get my *hopes* up?"[21] That could easily be many of us in the Wilderness. "God, did I ask you for that prophetic word or that promise that you gave me? Did I tell you to get my hopes up?" We need to keep the thought ever before us that we are only looking at one chapter in the totality of our lives. The end of the story has not been played out yet.

The end of the Shunammite's story, in the Bible, is that Elisha prayed over the boy and he came back to life! She went into the room where the boy was, fell at Elijah's feet, and took her son with her. She did not know this final part of the story in her Wilderness journey. All she knew was Elijah got her hopes up, then what seemed liked her blessing died. In the Wilderness this can be true for us as well. We have the courage to get our hopes up, but then what seems like a blessing *sent by God* "dies." It may be a job, a house, a promotion, or a business deal, but the end of our story has not been written yet. God can and will resurrect dead things!

Many times we cry out to God, "Do not get my hopes up. I have been down this road before and been tremendously disappointed." David, in the Bible, felt the same way. He prayed, "Day and night I have only tears for food, while my enemies continually taunt me, saying, 'Where is this God of yours?' My heart is breaking as I remember how it used to be. Why am I discouraged? Why is my heart so sad? I will put my hope in God! I will praise Him again—my Savior and my God."[22] It is easy to continue to look at that which was lost, especially when there seems to be *nothing* in front us to *move toward*. But we need to trust God that He truly does have something better for us, and that "He is a rewarder of those who diligently seek Him."[23]

Hope is the solid hook in the wall that faith hangs on to.

Hope is the solid hook in the wall that faith hangs on to. When we get down or depressed and lose hope, it is hard to have faith. Hope is the key ingredient for faith. God is a restorer of our hope so that we can have the faith to believe.

There was a man in the Bible who came to Jesus and said, "I believe, but help my unbelief."[24] That was a sincere prayer. He had a level of belief, but his unbelief was *negating* the faith he did have. We need to ask God to help us get rid of unbelief in our lives. Honesty before God is crucial. We can tell Him exactly where we are with our faith and any unbelief that we have, and ask Him for help. We will need hope and faith for the journey out of the Wilderness.

OUR PRAYER TO GOD

God,

Thank You that You are the restorer of my soul. Thank you for instilling hope in me so I can have the faith to continue the journey out of the Wilderness. I bind unbelief and ask for Your forgiveness in those areas of unbelief. I loose faith that You will perform Your Word, and it will come to pass. I ask You now for a Faith Releaser of (fill in the blank – i.e. penny story) to come and be an encouragement through this journey. I bind a spirit of hopelessness, and loose a spirit of hope. I pray that my faith rises to the occasion and produces all that it was meant to produce. I stand in confident expectation that You are who You say You are, and that You will do all that You said You would do. I come to You with an expectant heart and wait for the manifestation of Your promises everyday.

Amen

GOD'S PRAYER TO US

Dear Child,

I am a God who can restore lost hope. You will no longer have your hope deferred, but the desires of your heart will be fulfilled like a tree of life. Your hope in Me will flourish like a well watered tree planted by the water, that sends out its roots down by the stream.

I will grant the request of your heart for a Faith Releaser, but guard your heart against anyone or anything that is a Faith

*Deterrent. Do not allow unbelief to be a part of your life. Continue to trust and have faith that I am able **AND** I am willing to perform all that I have promised you. The key is to come to me with confident expectation, and make preparations to receive all that I have for you. That is great faith. That is the faith I want for you, My child. I love you so much. I want you to get to the place in your life where faith is a natural by-product of your day. Stay in peace. Stay in faith and allow me to move on your behalf. For I AM everything you need.*

Love,
The Great I AM

STUDY GUIDE

1. Pray and ask God to bring you a personal *Faith Releaser*—
   something that will be uniquely personal to you. Write
   it down in your journal and keep your eyes open for
   the manifestation! When you see it, thank God for His
   faithfulness.

2. Pray and ask God if there is anything in your life that
   is a *Faith Deterrent.* Whatever He shows you, ask Him
   how you are to deal with it. Write it down in your
   journal.

3. Invite the Holy Spirit to be a more prominent part
   of your life as your comforter and counselor. Listen
   for Him to speak to you each day. Then ask Him for
   the corresponding Scripture to back up what you
   are sensing. Write down in your journal what you
   are hearing from the Lord, and review it often to
   encourage yourself in faith.

END NOTES

1. Romans 10:17 (NKJV, Emphasis added).
2. John 10:27 (NASB).
3. Hebrews 13:8 (NIV).
4. John 14:12 (NLT).
5. Romans 5:5b (NASB).
6. Hebrews 11:6 (NIV).
7. Hebrews 3:19 (NKJV, Emphasis added).
8. Proverbs 18:21a (RSV).
9. Hebrews 11:1 (NASB, Emphasis added).
10. Hebrews 11:6 (NIV, Emphasis added).
11. Proverbs 23:18 (NIV).
12. Jeremiah 29:11 (NIV).
13. Romans 8:31 (NIV).
14. "Prisoner of War Syndrome." *The Free Dictionary by Farlex.* Retrieved from http://medical-dictionary.thefreedictionary.com.
15. Isaiah 55:8 (NIV).
16. Romans 4:20-21 (NLT, Emphasis added).
17. Psalm 84:11b (NIV).
18. Deuteronomy 8:7a (NIV).
19. Jeremiah 29:11b (NIV).
20. Habakkuk 2:3b (NASB).
21. See 2 Kings 4:8-28 (NIV).
22. Psalm 42:3,4a, 5, 6a (NLT).
23. Hebrews 11:6b (NKJV).
24. Mark 9:24 (NASB).

CHAPTER ELEVEN

DEEPER WITH THE LORD

"Your roots will grow down into God's love and keep you strong."
Ephesians 3:17b (NLT)

The Wilderness experience is designed to take us deeper with the Lord than we have ever been before—deeper in spiritual matters, deeper in the ways of God, and deeper in the revelations of His Spirit. During this time, we may feel like there is something over us, like a lid, preventing us from growing or moving forward. Before the Wilderness, we may have experienced a time of many open doors. Then all of a sudden it felt like all the doors slammed in our face. This is only a perceived lid that is over us to force us to go deeper with the Lord. The Scripture says, "He will be like a tree planted by the water that sends out its roots by the stream. It does not fear when heat comes; its leaves are always green. It has no worries in a year of *drought* and never fails to bear fruit."[1] We will be like a plant that has deep roots that lead to an underground stream.

A good example of this is the cactus. Two types of root systems help a cactus survive in the desert. The first is rather large and expansive, and is very close to the top of the soil. It expands outward and can quickly absorb any water that is on the surface because it is so close to the top of the soil. The other part of its root system is a very long, large root that goes straight down to reach the deep water in the ground. It goes down and hits a spring deep under the soil. It also gives the plant stability against the forces, like winds and storms. This is true for us in the Wilderness of our experience.

This perceived lid over us is actually making our main root go deeper into the soil until we hit the tap. Once we hit that tap, circumstances that come against us will not topple us over. Corrie Ten Boom, a holocaust survivor said, "The tree on the mountain takes whatever the weather brings. If it has any choices at all, it is in putting down roots as deeply as possible."[2]

When we hit that deep reservoir of water, there is a new found freedom that comes. When we hit that underground stream, then *no weapon* formed against will prosper and our lives line up with that truth, because it is now embedded into our spirit. When similar situations arise that have bothered us in the past, they do not bother us anymore, because we have been freed from them. When we are getting our water from an underground well, then flowing out of us is that with which we have been entrusted. We are no longer *needy* and always looking to others to pray for us on a daily basis as a *lifestyle*, but we are reaching out to others from a wholeness that was not there before this Wilderness experience.

Once we have tapped into the new stream, there are times of refreshing even in the midst of the most barren Wilderness. If we dig deep with the Lord, become transparent in His presence, and ask Him the *tough* questions, we reach a new-found level that goes far beyond anything we ever experienced before. We need to hold to the faith we profess and the hope which anchors it.[3]

If we dig deep in the Lord, we will not only take the high ground, but become a part of it. God will make our mountain stand firm. It is like the underground continental plates of the earth that are shifting. As the plates begin to shift, one plate is driven underneath another creating earthquakes and volcanoes. In these last days, I believe there is a shaking

> **If we dig deep in the Lord, we will not only take the high ground, but become a part of it.**

and a shifting in the Body of Christ that is taking place and the "plates" are moving. This shifting is forcing us to dig deep and go further than we have ever gone before in the Lord. It is driving us beyond basic Sunday School answers, or spoon-fed teachings on Sunday mornings. It is compelling us to dig deep into His Word.

The shifting produces volcanoes that begin to erupt and when they have cooled, mountains are formed. It is the fire of our situations that shifts our atmosphere and our lives. The heat of adversity creates something huge that jets us out further than we were before. This change needs to happen in order for us to rise to the level to which God is calling us. This shifting is necessary, but many times it looks like an eruption—an interruption of our schedules, plans, finances, or our personal goals. It is a time of realignment. "O Lord, when You favored me, You made my mountain stand firm. ... You turned my wailing into dancing; You removed my sackcloth (grieving) and clothed me with joy, that my heart may sing to You and not be silent."[4] In this eruption, we are not only taking the high-ground, we are becoming a part of it.

GOD MAKING US INTO DIAMONDS

As I was praying one day in my Wilderness experience, God gave me a picture of a miner sifting over and over at the same spot for diamonds. I saw an extremely valuable diamond in the wooden box screen, but it came with a lot of sifting. This is a good word picture describing how I felt in the Wilderness. I jokingly told

God, "If there is this much sifting going on, then please make it the Pink Panther diamond that comes to the surface." He is sifting and stirring up things in our lives to bring out the diamonds in us. The pressure in the Wilderness is forming us into diamonds. Sometimes the pressure in the Wilderness is meant for us, and sometimes it is for those around us.

There were times in the Wilderness when I took on things that were not meant for me. I stepped into situations I had no business going into. When I did this, a big crushing weight came on me so strongly that I felt suffocated. It was the heaviest thing I have ever felt in my entire life! But the weight was not meant for me.

Pressure is an interesting thing. It can crush one person, but can completely transform another. Geologists believe that diamond deposits were formed in the mantle of the earth. In regions called diamond stability zones, natural diamonds *form under immense pressure* and require very high temperatures. Diamonds formed and stored in these zones are delivered to the earth's surface during deep-source volcanic eruptions. These eruptions tear out pieces of the mantle and carry them to the surface.[5]

It is by digging down deep that we hit the tap to come up and take the high ground like never before. We not only *take* the high ground, but we become a *part* of the high ground because God's truth is now embedded in us and we have the faith to come out. We become diamonds on display for the world to see.

There is technology available today to turn a person's ashes into a diamond after they have died and been cremated. It is an expensive venture, but the diamonds are quite beautiful and come in many different shapes and colors. The process is to take the ashes of the deceased person, and under enormous pressure turn them into diamonds.

This is true for us in the Wilderness. God takes those things in our lives that have died, and under tremendous pressure forms diamonds out of them. We will sparkle and become His radiant bride through the ashes of things that have died in the Wilderness. God will "provide for those who grieve ... to bestow on them a crown of *beauty instead of ashes*, the oil of

> ## God will provide for those who grieve.

gladness instead of mourning, and a garment of praise instead of a spirit of despair."[6] God replaces the ashes, the mourning, and a spirit of despair, and gives us beauty, gladness, and praise. Like diamonds, which are very expensive to produce, there is a price to be paid in the Wilderness. But the cost is completely worth it, as we are transformed into His beautiful image.

CAN YOU SEE IT?

When we imagine the fulfillment of the promises God gave us, it brings both hope and faith for our journey out. The Israelites were always remembering Egypt and the things they missed. Did they forget that they were slaves? I cannot think of many things they really had in Egypt that were any better than in the Wilderness. They needed to stay focused and keep their eyes on the Promised Land.

What do we see? How much can we believe for right now? We need a starting point. Then God can help us to build it to a bigger and bigger vision, but at least we can start *somewhere*. In Jeremiah, God was training the prophet to visualize and practice his prophetic gifting. God said to Jeremiah, "What do you see Jeremiah?" He said, "I see the branch of an almond tree." The Lord said to him, "You have seen correctly, for I am watching to see that My Word is fulfilled."[7] The Lord asked him a second time what he saw and confirmed what he saw. Then God gave him the meaning attached to what he saw. It is interesting that God asked Jeremiah not only what he *saw*, but his *interpretation* of what he saw. This is important, both in the Wilderness and when visualizing the Promised Land. It is not only seeing those things that God is showing us, but knowing what *meaning* we are attaching to the things He shows us. God wants to help us see the promise, but He also wants to make sure our interpretation of the things we are going through is correct. Both need to be in alignment in our lives to move forward in faith.

In order to make it out of the Wilderness, our focus needs to be on the right things. Joshua and Caleb were focusing on the huge grapes they had seen in the Promised Land. The grapes were so large it took two men with a pole to carry them. *Supernatural fruit* was on the other side of their Wilderness experience. Joshua and Caleb believed, *even if no one else around them believed.* Big grapes, *not* big giants, was their report. The other spies were focusing on the big giants and not the enormous fruit in the Promised Land.

What are we focusing on in our Wilderness experience? Are we focusing on what God has showed us that is to come, or are we focusing on the giant circumstances in our life, such as debt, disappointment, our troubled marriage, or health challenges? At times we may not even know what God has promised or what to focus on. Simply ask God. He will direct us in the Bible to find verses we can stand on as His personal promises to us.

GOD GETS THE FINAL WORD

During one of the hardest parts of my Wilderness experience someone told me, "It is done!" As soon as they said this, God said to me in my spirit, "It may be *done*, but *I* am **not** *finished* yet!" This was something I had to be reminded of over and over. I was angry about all that had been lost in my Wilderness. I kept saying with bitterness of soul, "Well, this thing is *gone*, and that thing is *gone*. What is *done*—is *done*." But the Lord spoke very clearly and sternly to my heart and said, "Do not declare it *gone (done)*, because I am *not finished* yet!"

The word *done* means *to do* or *work*. The word *finished* (in Greek) means *to perform the last act which completes a process*. The Wilderness is a process and God is the only one that completes this process.

"God has the final word in our circumstances, not other people or the situation," my friend Treseen said. God is bigger than anyone else in our lives. We may have people in our lives telling us it is *done*, but God is *not finished* yet! It may look *gone*, *dead*, and *buried*, but He is the God of the

> **God has the final word in our circumstances, not other people.**

269

resurrection. **When Jesus died on the cross *man* said it was done, but *God* gets the final word and says when it is finished!** Death has been defeated and through Christ we can take the spoils of all that has been stolen. In our Wilderness experience it may seem like things in our situation are *done*, but God is not *finished* yet! He gets the final word.

His greatest work is yet to be revealed in our lives. The greatest manifestation of His glory is about to come. Hold on. The time is coming when "He will avenge us in the most peaceful way." God is ready to bring new life to our situation as we reach out and stand on His promises each day. "Did I not tell you if you believed, you will see the glory of God?"[8] Wait expectantly for your King to make a move with His mighty right hand of authority.

It looks the darkest right before the dawn. "No pit is so deep that He is not deeper still, with Jesus even in our darkest moments, the best remains and the very best is yet to be."[9] There are many examples of this *dark* period of time in the Bible. It is similar to the time after Christ died and it looked like all was lost. It is the three days between His death and His resurrection. It is the time between Joseph in jail and his release to stand before Pharaoh. It is the time between Lazarus dying and God resurrecting him. It is the time between David losing everything (all his family and possessions) at Ziglag and becoming king of Israel. It is the dark times of waiting between what "died" and what is yet to be "resurrected," when we need to stay strong in our faith.

Corrie Ten Boom also wrote, "When a train goes through a tunnel and it gets dark, you do not throw away the ticket and jump off. You sit still and trust the engineer."[10] Faith for the journey out of the Wilderness requires us to believe through the darkest times. What God has started, He will complete. I felt the Lord say to me, "I am the Lord, and I do not change my mind. I am a God of completion." Then He gave me the Scripture that says, "God is not a man, that He should lie, nor a son of man, that He should change His mind. Does He speak and then not act? Does He promise and not fulfill?"[11] We need to trust Him even when things around us do not make sense. He will complete what **He** started, not what someone else has started. God says, "I am with you and will watch over you wherever you go, and I will bring you back to this land. I will not leave you until I have done what I have promised you."[12]

When we believe God and take Him at His word, He will bring us faith that is anchored in hope to make it out. The Scripture says, "But then I will win her back once again. I will lead her into the desert and speak tenderly to her there. I will return her vineyards to her and transform the Valley of Trouble into a gateway of hope."[13] God will turn our valley of trouble into hopefulness so that we can have faith to journey out of the Wilderness.

The Bible says, "I will bring the blind by a way they did not know; I will lead them in paths they have not known. I will make *darkness light* before them, and crooked places straight. These things I will do for them, and not forsake them."[14]

God is bringing you to a deeper place with Him as you journey out of the Wilderness. Stay strong in the power of His might. You will make it out. Continue to trust. Continue to believe. Continue to walk so tightly with Him that nothing and no one can separate you in this journey together. He will bring you into your destiny and give you the hope you need for your faith to stand on. You will have the faith to journey **OUT** of this Wilderness, even on your toughest days!

OUR PRAYER TO GOD

God,

Thank You that through the pressure of my situation you are forming me into a diamond; one that is beautiful and completely captivating for the world to look on in wonder. Thank You that through "eruptions" in my life, Your truth is being embedded in me, and I am not only taking the high-ground, but I am becoming a part of it! I choose to go deeper in Your word and continue to believe. I will believe You even in the midst of my darkest hour, because You are a God of resurrection power. Now let death become life in Your resurrection power. My final story has not been told yet.

Holy Spirit, I welcome You into my life as part of the Trinity. I am open to You to move in a greater dimension, like never before. Speak to me as a counselor and a comforter. I choose to go deeper with You than I ever have before. I choose to have the faith to believe I will make it out of this Wilderness. And more than anything, I choose to stand on Your Word over my life everyday.

Amen

GOD'S PRAYER TO US

My Child,

The Wilderness is for those who want to go further in Me. Not everyone will go through a true Wilderness experience, but only those who want to go deeper with Me and see signs and wonders unfold. Yes, there will be many people who go through trials, but these are different from My Wilderness experience. Remember that this time in the Wilderness is not a punishment. It is an invitation to join Me in what I am about to do in your life, to expand you to receive what is coming. I know it came with a great price, but I am birthing something new in you. Continue on your journey, for I have set joy before you. You will not be the same person coming out of the Wilderness that you were going into it.

Know that I have the best in store for you. There is huge fruit that is being produced in your life right now, and your roots are going deep into Me. There is coming a time of shaking, but because your roots are so deep in Me, you will stand strong in My Word and in My promises. My love for you is great and I only want what is best for you. Continue in hope and faith and you WILL make it out. Stay strong in the journey and you WILL come into your own personal Promised Land that is filled to the brim with every good thing you desire.

Love,
The God of the Wilderness and of the Promised Land

STUDY GUIDE

1. Is there any situation in your Wilderness that you feel is "done"? Ask God if this was something that had to go, or if He is going to resurrect it. Write down in your journal what you feel the Lord is saying to you.

2. Is there anything in your life that looks like an "eruption" of your schedule, plans, finances, or personal goals? Ask God what He is doing, and how you can line up with what He is about to do.

3. Spend some extra time with the Lord this week reading His Word and in prayer. Make an effort to go deeper with Him as you journey out of this Wilderness time.

END NOTES

1. Jeremiah 17:8 (NIV).
2. Corrie Ten Boom, *Each New Day*, Revell, a division of Baker Publishing Group, Ada, MI 49301.
3. See Hebrews 6:19 (NIV).
4. Psalm 30:7a, 11-12a (NIV, Emphasis added).
5. Retrieved from http://geology.com/articles/diamonds-from-coal/.
6. Isaiah 61:3a (NIV, Emphasis added).
7. See Jeremiah 1:11-12 (NIV).
8. John 11:40b (NIV).
9. Corrie Ten Boom. Retrieved from http://www.goodreads.com/quotes/519705.
10. Corrie Ten Boom. Retrieved from http://www.goodreads.com/quotes/583815.
11. Numbers 23:19 (NASB).
12. Genesis 28:15 (NIV).
13. Hosea 2:14-15a (NLT).
14. Isaiah 42:16 (NKJV).

A SPECIAL PRAYER

This is a prophetic word from Marsha Burns,
Small Straws in a Soft Wind, September 6, 2010.

"I am bringing you into alignment on every level. It is My will to position you properly so that My purposes can be accomplished, and My kingdom established. You may not think that you, as an individual, have much to do with destiny. But everything you think, say, or do is vitally important to the spiritual condition of your sphere of influence. Be diligent to demonstrate the kingdom.

You have been repositioned as you have had to let go of many things that once meant everything to you. This has been for the purpose of establishing you in greater spiritual reality with renewed strength and vitality. You have stepped into a time of being reconnected to your spiritual roots, yet with refreshing revelation.

The days ahead will be filled with My glory in the practical and commonplace things of life as you maintain awareness and see

My manifest presence in unexpected ways. Walk in the Spirit and be available.

Events that left you reeling and trying to find stability and balance will now truly become a thing of the past as you begin to realize how insignificant it all was as compared with eternity and destiny. The power of My healing and restoration will become evident as you are able to release those who caused you pain. Forgiveness is essential to redemption.

I have established an altar in the heavenlies, in the realm of the Spirit, where you can bring all that concerns you, things you can do nothing about, and things you have absolutely no control over. Leave them with Me. Release your fear and anxiety. Nothing is impossible with Me. Come into that place of peace and rest, trusting Me in all things.

You feel like you have been cut off, but this cutting off has only been from those things that needed to be put aside at this time. You are like a tree that has been cut off and banded so that your spiritual roots could go deeper and you could become stronger. Let your roots go deeper in the Word, in revelation, and relationship to Me. The day of release will come in due season.

There are times when you feel totally disconnected and alone. This is because the enemy has lied to you and tried to isolate and weaken you, but that is not My design or plan for you. Now is the time to reconnect spiritually, first to Me, then to those who are Mine. Take the time and make the effort to re-establish yourself in divine connections and kingdom purpose.

Allow Me to take you forward inch by inch, step by step, without fear or worry. I am with you and will open doors that no man can shut and shut doors that no man can open. Trust Me with your future. I have already proven to you over and over again that I alone am your place of security," says the Lord.

Stand strong in the Lord and in the power of His might. You will make it through to the other side. Continue to trust. Continue to believe. Continue to walk with your Savior, and He will uplift you with His mighty right hand. You will have the faith to make it out...even in your roughest days!

CHAPTER TWELVE

THE GOD OF THE WILDERNESS

"If you confess with your mouth, 'Jesus is Lord,' and believe in your heart that God raised Him from the dead, you will be saved."
Romans 10:9 (NIV)

It is truly hard to go through the Wilderness with God—without Him it is impossible. I cannot imagine facing life's difficulties without Jesus. There are many heartaches and losses in the Wilderness. It may be the loss of a job or a marriage. It may be the heartache of bankruptcy, the burden of wayward children, or grieving the loss of a dear friend or family member. Know that God is in the midst of your own personal Wilderness journey.

Many people view God through the eyes of their own earthly fathers. If their father was mean and abusive, they view God as a driven task master who wants to punish them when they make a mistake. If their father was critical, they view God as wanting perfection from them before they can know Him. If their father was aloof and not caring, they view God as high-in-the-sky and not really interested in their life, and they end up always feeling alone. All these views are *FALSE.* They are not the true nature and character of God.

God is GOOD ALL THE TIME *no matter what the circumstances.* God's nature and character never changes. *We* have a natural tendency to change how we view God based on the circumstances we are going through. He *NEVER* changes. He is *all in* and has been *all in* for a very long time. God loves you with an unconditional love and cannot be *more in* than He is already. He sent His son, Jesus, to die on the cross over 2,000 years ago. He "put all his chips on the table" when He did this. He took a big risk by being *all in* because He gave all of us a free choice. We can choose to be *all in* with Him or we can fold and walk away.

KNOWING GOD

If you do not know Him today, this may seem foreign to you. All that can change if you *confess* with your mouth and *believe* with your heart that Jesus is Lord. I extend this invitation to you today to make Jesus a part of your life. There is no fancy prayer to pray—just be open and honest and ask Jesus to come into your life. He died for your sins to redeem you and paid the price for your eternal soul. He loves you more than you can ever imagine, and you are not alone. You are not forgotten in this Wilderness and He knows you by name. His nature and character is love. You have a hope. You have a future. God loves you beyond your wildest dreams. Let Him into your heart and you will never be the same.

This is a prayer that you can pray to receive Jesus into your life. It is *not* some special magical prayer. You can actually pray anything you want to pray and God will hear you and answer you. You can pray to a wonderful and *LIVING* God who will speak to you every day! This prayer below will help you get started.

Dear God,

Thank You for sending your Son, Jesus, to die on the Cross for my sins. Thank You for laying it all on the line 2,000 years ago for me, and that You are all in. I choose to be all in. I give you my heart and soul. I give You my mind. I choose in simple childlike faith to believe. No matter what my circumstances look like, I believe. God, I am all in and I trust You. I ask You, Holy Spirit, to come into my life and be my comforter and counselor. I invite You to lead me every day. As You guide me into all truth, I will follow You all the days of my life. Help me walk out this life as a believer in Jesus.

Amen

If you prayed this prayer, the Bible says the angels are rejoicing.[1] They are throwing a party in heaven because of your decision. Your next step is to get a Bible (the New Living Translation is good start) and simply begin reading. There is no secret formula for how or what order you read it in. The story of the Wilderness is found in the second book of the Bible called *Exodus.* The story of the Promised Land is found in the sixth book of the Bible called *Joshua.* The story of Jesus is found in the Gospels of Matthew, Mark, Luke, and John (the first books in the New Testament). Those are all great places to start this wonderful adventure. Reading your Bible every day is very important to your growth, and one way in which God will speak to you. The other way He will speak to you is by His Holy Spirit. Ask the Holy Spirit to guide you each day as you read His Word.

When you pray to God, *expect* Him to talk back to you. In a conversation one person talks and

> **When you pray to God, expect Him to talk back to you.**

the other person responds. *Expect* to hear Him. Wait until you do. It is not a religious exercise that He wants from us, but a living, breathing relationship with Him. Be honest in your prayers to Him. He can handle it.

The next step is to find a local church to attend. Find a Christian church where you feel loved and where you feel God is alive. Make sure the church believes in the power of the Holy

Spirit. You will be looking for a church that is full of grace and forgiveness, not one where the preacher is condescending or condemning, and not one that is "rule-based." Once you get there, volunteer to help in one of their ministries. This is a great way to meet people and get connected right away. Connecting with like-minded people is very important.

COMING BACK HOME

If you are a Christian already and you feel far away from God, pray and ask Him to speak to you in this time in the Wilderness. God has sent His Holy Spirit to speak to us in our hearts and to be our counselor. For many years I grew up in a church that said they believed in the Holy Spirit, but basically stripped Him of His power.

I prayed and asked the Lord to give me more of the Holy Spirit in my life. I did not want to be afraid of Him. I declared over that year, "The Year of the Holy Spirit" and I said, "Have your way with me." After I did that, I have heard the Lord through the Holy Spirit more than I ever had in my entire life. I wish I had done this earlier! Letting go of my fear of the Holy Spirit and wanting more of Him in my life has allowed me a more open dialog with the Lord. I am completely thrilled and excited about the Holy Spirit now! I pray that as you continue to make the journey out of the Wilderness you will keep God in the center of your life and submit to His will. You WILL make it into your own personal Promised Land.

Do you feel like you want to hear more from God during this Wilderness journey? Here is a prayer that can help you get started:

Dear God,

I want to hear from You during these days in the Wilderness. I am sorry that I walked away in my grief. I want to come closer to You and make You the center of my life. I ask You, Holy Spirit, to become more real to me than You have ever been before. Speak to me as I read my Bible. Illuminate promises that I can stand on and meditate on in my journey out of the Wilderness. Thank You for being my comforter. I know You will be there during my times of loss. Guide me into my Promised Land. I give my life to You Jesus and say, "I am all in!"

Amen

END NOTE

1. See Luke 15:7

Please share your "God Stories" with us on the website. Talking about your Wilderness journey will bring encouragement to others who are still journeying through.

For more information on resources and events, please refer to our website:

www.WildernessToPromisedLand.com